# Reader's Digest
# Home
# Safety &
# Security
# DIY Manual

# Reader's Digest
# Home Safety & Security
## DIY Manual

**Expert guidance on safety and security in the home**

Published by
The Reader's Digest Association Limited
London • New York • Sydney • Montreal

# Contents

# About this book

Each year in the UK more than 2.7 million people find themselves in hospital accident and emergency departments as a result of an accident in the home; 4,000 people die. The advice in this book will help you to keep safe at home when doing DIY or just going about your daily business. It will also help you to make your home secure against intruders and protect your belongings from theft.

The four main causes of accidents in the home are falls; accidental poisoning; drowning, suffocation or choking (perhaps as the result of a fire); and fire or burns. On pages 8–9 you will find an example of what to keep in your household first aid kit so that you are equipped to deal with the most common minor injuries. You will also find more detailed, step-by-step first aid instructions throughout Chapter One, so that you can deal safely and confidently with more serious accidents and injuries, such as poisoning, electric shock, burns and smoke inhalation. Read these pages now (18, 27, 50–52 and 58–59), so that you are prepared and ready to act in an emergency.

## Working safely and staying safe at home

Chapter One is all about safety. You'll find helpful advice on working safely with gas, electrical and water systems around the home and on spotting potential faults and hazards. Find out what to do in an emergency and how to stop a simple fault, such as a burst pipe from turning into a bigger disaster. Pages 12–40 show you all you need to know.

### Know what to do in a fire

Pages 41–53 tell you what you can do to protect your home against fire, by fitting smoke alarms – and using them – and by keeping simple fire-fighting equipment close to hand, such as a fire blanket in the kitchen or a fire extinguisher in the hall or garage. Find out how to spot the tell-tale signs of an electrical fault that could develop into a fire and follow some simple tips around the house to prevent fires from starting. Check your house for the top ten fire hazards around the home, listed on page 53 and make sure that everyone in the household, including children, knows what to do and how best to escape in the event of a fire – read pages 47–49 so that you are all prepared, but don't have nightmares!

### Avoiding accidents

Accidental poisoning is the second biggest cause of household accidents and pages 55–59 show you how to assess your home for dangers and give you clear advice on how to deal swiftly with the victim of a poisoning incident.

Accidents with power tools – inside and in the garden – and ladders are also common and can be serious. Follow the advice on pages 60–67 for staying safe outdoors.

Pages 68–77 take you room-by-room around the house, assessing potential dangers and offering safety tips and advice. You'll find advice on storing knives and cleaning products safely in the kitchen, on minimising the risk of falls or scalding in the bathroom, on avoiding fires and accidents with fires in the living room, making your stairs, hall and landing safe and more.

# Top tips for a secure home

Chapter Two tells you all you need to know to keep your home and your belongings safe and secure. Pages 80–81 help you to look at your house critically and spot weak points in its security and opportunities for burglars to help themselves to your things. Learn to think like a thief and never leave ladders or garden or DIY tools where they could be used to break in.

## Locks and latches for doors and windows

Fitting appropriate locks and latches to doors and windows is the first step in home security and pages 82–95 show you how.

There is expert advice on all the different lock options available and help choosing the right one for you, and clear, illustrated, step-by-step instructions for fitting them.

## Security systems

You'll also find advice on electrical home security systems, from door entry systems where you can see and speak to whoever is calling to burglar alarms and CCTV systems for monitoring your house and garden. Or you may just want to fit a simple wall light outside the front door, or a security light that comes on when someone approaches. From the simple to the sophisticated, find out more on pages 98–107.

You can reduce your risk of being burgled and increase the chances of getting your belongings back if they are taken by marking your valuables with special pens, punching information into metal objects, applying microdot markings and more. Page 108 tells you how.

## Security outside the house

Pages 110–117 are packed with tips for keeping your shed and garage secure and for preventing thefts of bicycles, cars, motorbikes, caravans, boats and trailers, whether they are parked on your driveway or outside the house, or away from the home. Car crime – the theft of cars themselves and of property left in cars while they are parked – makes up nearly 20 per cent of all recorded crimes, so find out what you can do to protect yourself from the distress and inconvenience involved.

## Empty houses

Unoccupied properties make easy targets for burglars; pages 118–9 have lots of tips for keeping your property safe while you are away on holiday, from remembering to cancel your milk delivery to asking a trusted neighbour to push letters and newspapers that are poking out of the letterbox through your door and to go in every few days to pick up the post and move it away from the doormat.

And pages 120-1 tell you all you need to know if you would like to set up a Neighbourhool Watch scheme in your area.

## Modern threats

You'll also find tips for avoiding and dealing with some particularly modern threats to personal security, such as dealing with bogus callers at the door and protecting yourself from identity theft or online crimes.

# First aid kit

Every home and car should carry a well-stocked first aid kit which is checked regularly – supplies should be replenished when they are used or become out of date. Keep the kit in a clean, dry place where it is readily accessible when needed.

You can buy first aid kits from most pharmacists, or you can make up your own, provided that you keep it in a container with a well-fitting lid, that is both clean and watertight. A first aid kit should be clearly marked so that anyone can find it easily in an emergency.

## BASIC CONTENTS

- adhesive dressings (plasters)
- sterile dressings
- bandages in various sizes including triangular bandages
- dressing tape
- disposable latex gloves
- safety pins or bandage clips
- eye pads
- antiseptic cream or spray
- cotton gauze swabs
- cotton wool for padding (not to be placed directly on a wound)
- notebook and pencil
- tweezers

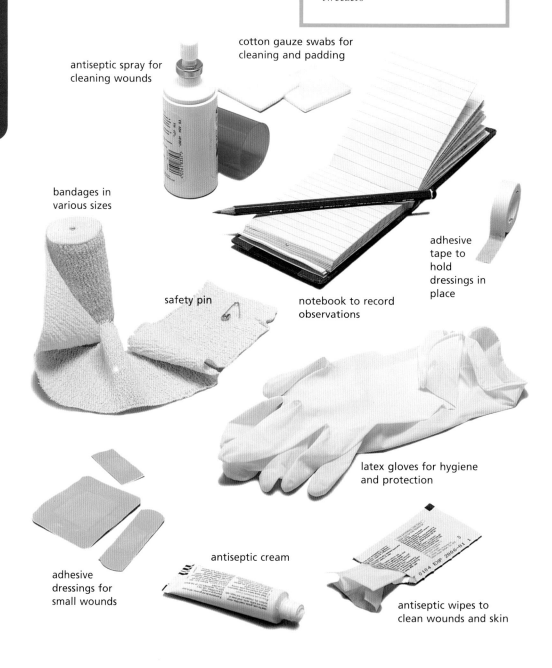

antiseptic spray for cleaning wounds

cotton gauze swabs for cleaning and padding

bandages in various sizes

adhesive tape to hold dressings in place

safety pin

notebook to record observations

latex gloves for hygiene and protection

adhesive dressings for small wounds

antiseptic cream

antiseptic wipes to clean wounds and skin

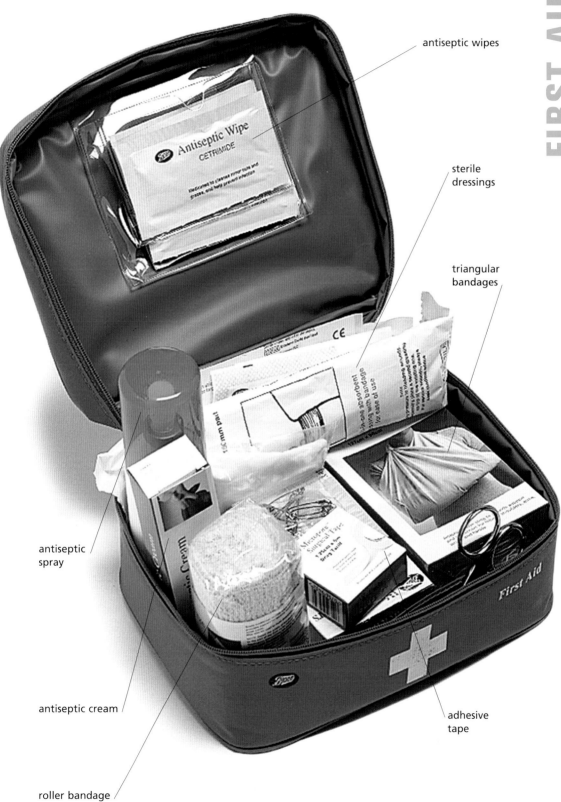

antiseptic wipes

sterile
dressings

triangular
bandages

antiseptic
spray

antiseptic cream

adhesive
tape

roller bandage

# Safety

# Electrical safety

Every year, there are around 10 deaths and 750 injuries in the UK as a result of faulty electrical work. Follow these safety precautions to keep yourself safe when using electrical appliances or working with or near electric circuits. See pages 16–17 for Wiring Regulations governing electrical safety in the home.

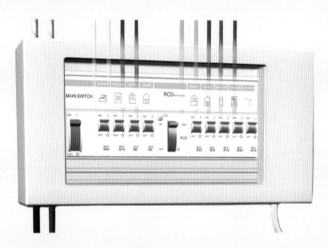

**Isolate mains circuits** at the consumer unit (above) by switching off the miniature circuit breakers (MCBs) or removing the circuit fuses before carrying out any work on the house wiring.

**Uncoil extension leads fully** before using them. If the lead is powering any appliance with a heating element, check that the flex rating is suitable for the appliance wattage.

**Always unplug appliances** from the mains before attempting any repair work on them.

**Do not overload socket outlets** – either mechanically, by using adaptors, or electrically, by plugging in too many high-wattage appliances. If you are using a four or six-way adaptor, refer to the label on the back of the adaptor to check the maximum load.

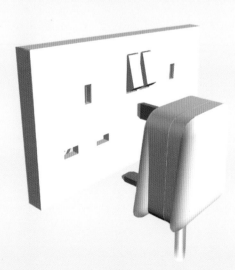

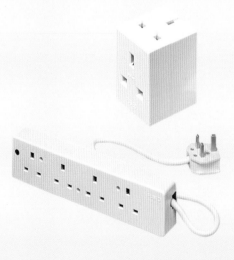

**Check appliance plugs and flexes** regularly for damage, cuts or other signs of wear. Replace damaged parts at the earliest possible opportunity.

**Replace blown circuit fuses** using fuse wire or cartridge fuses of the correct rating (see pages 22–23). Never use any other metallic object to repair a fuse.

**Out of doors**, plug any power tool being used into a residual current device (RCD) adaptor (right).

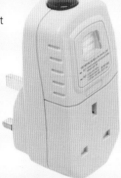

**Check there are earth connections** for all appliances and wiring accessories that need them, and earth all metal pipework and plumbing fittings. The only situation where an earth connection is not needed is in the flex to a non-metallic lampholder or to power tools and portable appliances that are double-insulated.

**Use a cable detector** (right) to locate hidden cables and pipes before making holes for wall fixings.

**Keep water and electricity apart**
Never plug in appliances or operate electrical switches with wet hands. Never take an electrical appliance into the bathroom, even if the flex is long enough. Never use electrical equipment outside the house in wet conditions.

## TRADE ORGANISATIONS

**Electrical Contractors Association**
ESCA House
34 Palace Court
London W2 4HY
020 7313 4800

www.eca.co.uk

**National Inspection Council for Electrical Installation Contracting (NICEIC)**
Vintage House
37 Albert Embankment
London SE1 7UJ
020 7564 2323

www.niceic.org.uk

**Institution of Electrical Engineers (IEE)**
Savoy Place
London WC2R 0BL
020 7240 1871

www.iee.org.uk

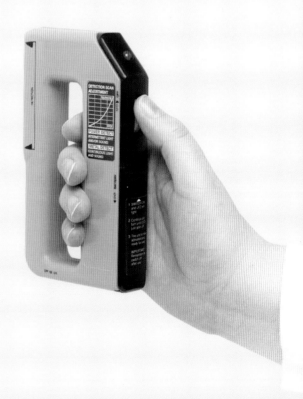

# Does your wiring need replacing?

If your home has an old wiring system it may be unsafe. Also, it may not be able to cope with the demands of all the electrical appliances you want to use. Having it rewired to modern standards is the only solution.

## Old main switches and fuse boxes

Check the main fuse board. Look for cables from the meter going to a metal box with a main on/off switch for the installation. There may be separate switched fuse boxes for each circuit.

Inside the fuse boxes there may be circuit fuses in porcelain holders. Such a system is old and likely to be highly unsafe. It should be replaced. Replacement is especially important if each circuit has two fuses: the system could be lethal.

## Old light switches

Round brass or Bakelite light switches mounted on wooden blocks are signs of a lighting system that is more than 50 years old. The lighting circuits should be rewired with new cable and fittings as soon as possible.

## Old wiring – new fittings

You may have a system where the old rubber-insulated cables remain, but the switches and sockets have been replaced by modern ones. Look at the circuit cables where they emerge from the fuse box. If you find old cables, have them checked by an electrician, and plan to have the system rewired as soon as possible.

## Round-pin sockets

If you have old-style round-pin sockets, your wiring system is likely to be 50 or more years old. It should be completely rewired without delay for safety reasons.

# Tools for wiring work

Many of the jobs involved in wiring are non-electrical in nature – lifting floorboards, say. But for the electrical work, some special tools are essential.

**Torch** Choose one with a sturdy stand, or clip-on fitting. A powerful torch will light up work under floors and in lofts. Keep a supply of spare batteries or, better still, choose a torch with a rechargeable battery pack.

**Wire cutters** A pair of 125mm or 150mm wire cutters will cut cable and flex, and trim cores to length.

**Wire strippers** The adjustable blades will strip the insulation from cores of different sizes in cable and flex without damaging the conductors inside.

**Circuit continuity tester** With a simple battery-powered tester you can check the continuity of circuits and whether a socket outlet is on a ring main circuit or on a spur.

**Pliers** A pair of 150mm electrician's pliers is useful for twisting cable conductor cores together prior to insertion into terminals. The cutting jaws can also be used for cutting cable and flex.

**Tester screwdriver** An insulated screwdriver with a 3mm blade is used for tightening terminal screws in plugs and other wiring accessories. A bulb in the handle lights up if the tip touches a live terminal or conductor.

**Knife** A sharp knife will cut through thick cable sheath and flex sheath.

**Insulated screwdriver** A larger screwdriver with an insulating sleeve on the shaft is useful for undoing and tightening plug screws and the screws fixing accessory faceplates to their mounting boxes.

# Wiring regulations

Since January 2005, all new domestic wiring work in England and Wales must comply with the requirements of a new section of the Building Regulations. Part P, entitled Electrical Safety, covers the design, installation, inspection and testing of electrical work in the home. It applies to both professional and DIY electrical work.

## What you need to know:

**1** You can still do your own wiring work, but it must be inspected, tested and certified by a professional electrician.

**2** Any minor work that is not on a fixed electrical installation (for example, lamps and other appliances that can be unplugged) does not need approval.

**3** You must notify your local authority building control department before you start certain major wiring jobs and pay a fee for inspection and testing when the job is completed.

## Getting approval

DIY wiring work is still permitted following the introduction of Part P. You will be able to do minor work without approval on any electrical equipment that can be unplugged and moved around, for example, changing a plug or a flex on a lamp. But any work carried out on a fixed electrical installation (for example, wiring, sockets, ceiling roses, fuse boxes, light switches and fused connection units) must be inspected and tested by a 'competent person' when you have completed the job to ensure that it complies with the new regulations. This means calling in a professional electrician (see Employing an electrician, below right) who will inspect and test your work and then issue you with a Minor Electrical Installation Works Certificate if it is satisfactory.

Depending on the scale of the work involved, you may also have to notify your local authority building control department. This involves submitting a building notice to the department before you start work, and paying a building control fee to have the work inspected and tested and the relevant certificates issued when you have completed it.

## Exempt jobs

Some minor DIY wiring jobs do not need to be notified to the local authority. These include:

- Replacing existing wiring accessories, such as switches, socket outlets and ceiling roses.
- Replacing their mounting boxes.
- Replacing a single circuit cable that has been damaged by, for example, impact, fire or rodent attack.
- Adding new lighting points and switches to an existing lighting circuit, unless the work is in a kitchen or bathroom (see 'Jobs that must be notified', top right).
- Adding new socket outlets or fused spurs to an existing ring main or radial circuit, unless the work is in a kitchen or bathroom (see 'Jobs that must be notified', top right).

The work must still be inspected and tested on completion by a professional electrician – but not necessarily one registered with the 'Competent Person Scheme' (see right).

## Jobs that must be notified

Any other wiring jobs you carry out must be notified to your local building control department before you start work. These include:

• The installation of any new indoor circuit, such as one supplying an electric shower or a home extension.
• The installation of any new outdoor circuit, such as one supplying garden lighting or an outbuilding.
• Any new wiring work in a kitchen or bathroom. This includes the addition to an existing circuit of new lighting points, socket outlets or fused spurs, the installation or upgrading or equipotential bonding, and the installation of electric under-floor heating. But replacement of existing equipment (see left) in either type of room is exempt from notification.
• The installation of extra-low-voltage lighting circuits. But the installation on existing lighting circuits of pre-assembled extra-low-voltage light fittings with CE approval is exempt.

The local authority will inspect your work for a fee of around £100–£200. If you are in any doubt as to whether the work you plan to do requires notification, contact your local authority building control department for advice.

## Employing an electrician

You may decide to employ a professional electrician to carry out future wiring work for you. He or she must still follow all the procedures set out in Part P, and ensure that the work complies with the Wiring Regulations (BS7671).

It is recommended that you use an electrician who is registered with the 'Competent Person Scheme'. For minor electrical work, a registered electrician will issue you with a Minor Electrical Installation Works Certificate when the job has been completed. For major electrical work, a registered electrician is not required to notify the local authority. When the work is completed you will receive a Building Regulations Self-certification Certificate and an Electrical Installation Certificate.

You can use an electrician who is not registered with the 'Competent Person Scheme' but they must be qualified and registered with a recognised trade body such as NICEIC (see right). He or she can issue you with the same certificates but must notify the local authority before carrying out any major electrical work.

## New cable core colours

In 2006, the colours of the insulation around individual cable cores changed, and the new cable must now be used for all new fixed wiring work. This change was introduced as part of a process of product harmonisation across the European Union, some 37 years after flex core colours were changed from red and black to brown and blue.

When you have used the new cable to alter or extend an existing wiring installation, you must place a warning notice to this effect at the fuse board or consumer unit. Its wording is as follows:

---

### Caution

This installation has wiring colours to two versions of BS7671. Great care should be taken before undertaking extension, alteration or repair that all conductors are correctly identified.

---

When using two-core-and-earth cable with the new core colours, remember:

new brown = old red
new blue = old black

### Useful contacts
• Local Authority Building Control
020 7641 8737
www.labc-services.co.uk
• National Inspection Council for Electrical Installation Contracting (NICEIC)  020 7564 2323
www.niceic.org.uk
• Electrical Contractors Association (ECA)
020 7313 4800 www.eca.co.uk
• For further details on Part P visit
www.partp.co.uk
www.odpm.gov.uk
• If you are interested in qualifying to become a 'competent person', visit
www.techniquetraining.co.uk

# Electric shock

**If someone receives an electric shock, cut off the source of electricity before doing anything else.**

## Domestic-voltage shock

You can get a shock when electrical equipment has a fault, such as a damaged flex, or when it isn't used safely, such as handling an appliance with wet hands.

**1** Never touch the victim until you are certain that contact with the electric current has been broken, or you could be electrocuted yourself. Switch off the power, at the mains if possible, then disconnect the appliance from the power point.

**2** If you cannot switch the current off, stand on some insulating material – wood, rubber, plastic or thick paper. Use a non-metallic pole to push the current source clear or pull the victim away by a loop of rope if you can, or by tugging on clothing.

> ### HELPFUL TIP
>
> If the skin has been burned, flood the affected area with cold water for at least ten minutes, then apply a cold compress.
>
>

**3** If the victim is unconscious, **call an ambulance immediately**. Start CPR (cardiopulmonary resuscitation) if necessary. If the victim is breathing and has a pulse, look for burns on the skin and cool them with cold water.

---

### ✚ FIRST AID

Take prompt action if any of the following occurs:
- Burns at the site of entry and discharge of electric current
- Difficulty breathing
- Collapse and unconsciousness
- No pulse

**Do not touch the victim until the current has been disconnected.**

---

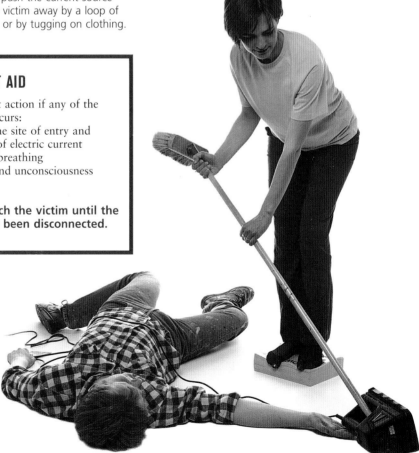

Use something wooden, such as a broom handle or chair leg, to break the electrical contact.

# Electrical emergencies

Warning: the main on-off switch on your consumer unit disconnects only the fuses or miniature circuit breakers (MCBs) and the cables leading out from it to the household circuits. It does NOT disconnect the cables entering via the meter from the service cable. Do not tamper with these cables. They are always live at mains voltage.

## Fire in an appliance

1 If a plug-in appliance is on fire, switch the appliance off at the socket outlet and pull out the plug.

2 If a fixed appliance with no plug is on fire, turn it off at the wall switch if you can, or at the main switch on the consumer unit (see below).

3 Do not use water on an electrical fire. Smother the fire with a rug or blanket, or use a dry-powder fire extinguisher.

4 Get the appliance checked (and repaired if possible) by an expert before you use it again.

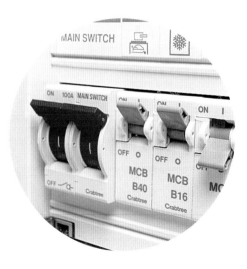

## Smell of overheating

1 If you smell burning from an appliance, turn off the switch at the socket and pull out the plug. If it is a fixed appliance with no plug, turn off its wall switch or the main switch at the consumer unit. Turn off the appliance switch. Have the appliance checked by an expert.

2 If the smell comes from a socket or plug, turn off the main switch at the consumer unit. If the plug is hot, let it cool before unplugging it. Check its connections, including fuse contacts, and examine the flex for damage and replace as necessary. If the socket is hot, check it for faulty connections and renew as necessary.

## No electricity

1 If you have a power cut and neighbouring houses are also without power, there is a mains supply failure. Call the 24-hour emergency number under 'Electricity' in the phone book.

2 If your system is protected by a whole-house residual current device (RCD), check whether it has switched itself off. Try to switch it on again if it has.

3 If it will not switch on, the fault is still present on the system. Call an electrician to track it down and rectify it.

4 If you do not have an RCD and your house is the only one without power, there may be a fault in your supply cable or your main supply fuse may have blown. Do not touch it. Report the power failure as above.

## Minor emergencies

1 If one appliance fails to work, unplug it and check its plug, fuse and flex; renew them as necessary. If the appliance still fails to work, plug it in a different socket outlet to test it. If it works, the problem is with the original socket; if not, have the appliance repaired.

2 If all lights or appliances on one circuit stop working, switch off at the consumer unit and check the circuit fuse (see pages 22–23). If it is sound, there may be a fault in the circuit cable. Call in an electrician to track it down and rectify it.

# Finding fault with the electrical system

Your electrical system can fail at several different levels. The cause may be something as simple as a blown plug fuse or faulty appliance, or there may be a fault in your circuit wiring. Follow the flow chart below to help you to diagnose the problem and work out how to fix it.

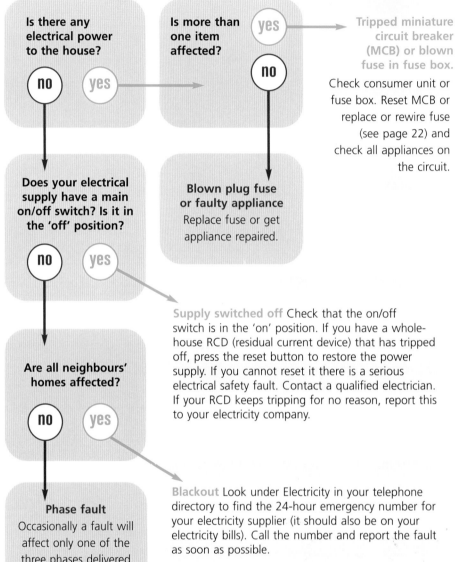

**Is there any electrical power to the house?**

no / yes

**Is more than one item affected?**

yes / no

**Tripped miniature circuit breaker (MCB) or blown fuse in fuse box.**

Check consumer unit or fuse box. Reset MCB or replace or rewire fuse (see page 22) and check all appliances on the circuit.

**Does your electrical supply have a main on/off switch? Is it in the 'off' position?**

no / yes

**Blown plug fuse or faulty appliance**

Replace fuse or get appliance repaired.

**Supply switched off** Check that the on/off switch is in the 'on' position. If you have a whole-house RCD (residual current device) that has tripped off, press the reset button to restore the power supply. If you cannot reset it there is a serious electrical safety fault. Contact a qualified electrician. If your RCD keeps tripping for no reason, report this to your electricity company.

**Are all neighbours' homes affected?**

no / yes

**Blackout** Look under Electricity in your telephone directory to find the 24-hour emergency number for your electricity supplier (it should also be on your electricity bills). Call the number and report the fault as soon as possible.

**Phase fault**

Occasionally a fault will affect only one of the three phases delivered from local substations, so power continues to be supplied to some neighbouring houses. Call the emergency number of your electricity supplier and report the fault.

---

## ELECTRICAL EMERGENCY ACTION

• If anyone receives a minor shock from an appliance, stop using it and have it checked by an expert.
• If someone receives a major shock, turn off the current immediately at the consumer unit. Refer to the guidelines on pages 18–19.

## FAULT DIAGNOSIS

### MILD SHOCK FROM METAL-CASED DEVICE

Earth fault within item Contact a qualified repairer. This fault should have tripped an RCD, so test yours, or have one fitted.

### NO POWER

MCB tripped Turn off appliances, reset switch and identify faulty device by unplugging all appliances, then reconnecting them one by one.

Whole house RCD tripped Reset RCD. If reset is impossible, call a qualified electrician.

Local power failure Check neighbouring buildings to verify, and report power failure to your electricity company.

Service fuse blown Call electricity company immediately to replace.

### MCB IN CONSUMER UNIT TRIPS REGULARLY

Circuit overload Caused by plugging in too many high-wattage appliances at once. Make sure that you don't overload a circuit – maximum wattage is 7kW.

Faulty device on circuit If an MCB trips when a specific appliance is used, unplug it and have it checked. If an MCB trips periodically, plug in one appliance at a time to find the faulty appliance. Then have it repaired.

# Choosing the right fuse

Always use the correct fuse for the job in hand. NEVER use any other metallic object or material in place of a blown fuse in order to restore power to a circuit or appliance. Doing so would remove the protection the fuse provides, and could allow an electrical fire to start or result in someone receiving a potentially fatal electric shock.

**Fuse wires**
If your consumer unit has rewirable fuses, use 5amp wire for a lighting circuit, 15amp wire for an immersion heater circuit, and 30amp wire for a ring main circuit or a circuit to a cooker rated at up to 12kW.

### Cartridge fuses

5A Use for a lighting circuit

15A Use for a storage heater or immersion heater circuit.

20A Use for a 20amp radial power circuit.

30A Use for a ring main circuit or a 30amp radial power circuit.

45A Use for a cooker or shower circuit.

# Changing a fuse in a consumer unit

If you still have circuit fuses, keep spare fuses or fuse wire to hand for instant repairs if a fuse 'blows'. For safety's sake, consider getting the fuse board replaced with a modern consumer unit.

## Mending a rewirable fuse

1 Turn off the main on/off switch in the consumer unit. On an older system it may be in a separate enclosure near the meter. Remove or open the cover over the fuse carriers.

2 Pull out each fuse carrier in turn to find out which has blown. Scorch marks often show this, or simply a break in the wire.

3 If a power circuit is affected, switch off and unplug all the appliances on the circuit. If it is a lighting circuit, turn off all the light switches. If you do not switch everything off, the mended fuse is likely to blow again immediately you turn the main switch back on. Replace the fuse wire (right).

## Replacing the fuse wire

1 Loosen the two terminal screws and remove any pieces of old wire. Cut a new piece of fuse wire of the correct amp rating, long enough to cross the carrier and go round both screws.

2 Wind the wire clockwise round one screw and tighten the screw.

3 Pass the wire across the bridge or thread it through the holder. If you are unsure about how the wire runs in the carrier, examine one of the intact fuses.

4 Wind the wire clockwise round the second screw. Make sure there is a little slack in the wire so that it will not snap and then tighten the screw.

5 Replace the fuse carrier in the consumer unit. Close the cover and restore the power by turning on the main switch.

## Checking the circuit

Look for damage on the appliances, lights and flexes that were in use on the circuit when it failed. Make repairs if necessary, then switch on the appliances or lights one at a time. Check that you are not overloading the circuit with too many high-wattage appliances. Overloading is the likeliest cause of the blown fuse. If the fuse blows again, call an electrician.

## TYPES OF REWIRABLE FUSE CARRIER

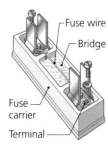

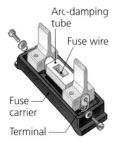

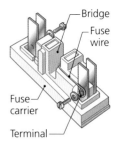

**Bridged fuse**
The wire runs from one terminal to the other over a plug of white arc-damping material. The carrier is ceramic.

**Protected fuse**
Between the terminals the wire runs through a porcelain arc-damping tube. The carrier is tough plastic.

**Fuse between humps**
The unprotected wire passes round humps between one terminal and the other. The carrier is ceramic.

## Replacing a cartridge fuse

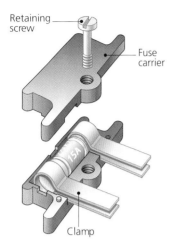

Retaining screw

Fuse carrier

Clamp

---

**Tools** *Insulated screwdriver; fuse tester.*

**Materials** *Cartridge fuses.*

---

**1** Turn off the main switch on the consumer unit.

**2** Find out which fuse has blown: take out each fuse carrier in turn so you can test the cartridge.

**3** Prise the cartridge gently from the clamps. Some carriers are in two halves and the screw holding them together has to be removed to give access to the cartridge.

**4** Test the cartridge with a fuse tester (see right). Remove only one carrier at a time. Test its cartridge and replace the carrier before removing the next one for inspection and testing.

**5** When you have traced the blown fuse, replace the cartridge with a new one of the amp rating shown on the carrier.

**6** As with a rewirable fuse, switch off all appliances or lights on the affected circuit. Replace the fuse carrier, close the box and turn on the main switch. Check the circuit in the same way as for rewirable fuses.

## Checking a miniature circuit breaker

If the consumer unit is fitted with miniature circuit breakers (MCBs) instead of circuit fuses, it is immediately clear which circuit is affected. The switch will be in the 'off' position or the button will have popped out.

**1** Turn off the main switch on the consumer unit.

**2** Switch off all appliances or light switches on the affected circuit. If you do not do this, the MCB may trip off again when you reset it.

**3** Push the MCB switch to the 'on' position or push in the button. Then turn the main switch back on.

**4** Check the circuit in the same way as for a rewirable fuse (left).

### TESTING A FUSE

You can buy an inexpensive tester that will tell you if a cartridge fuse has blown. Some types can also check flat batteries and blown light bulbs.

# Gas safety

Mains gas will not poison you, but it can explode if it leaks and is ignited. It can also kill indirectly if it is not burned safely and under controlled conditions in a gas fire, boiler or water heater.

Follow these guidelines to ensure that you always use gas safely.

**1** Never attempt DIY work on your gas pipes, fittings or appliances: this is illegal. Always call in a CORGI-registered fitter to do the work.

**2** If you smell gas turn off the supply at the main on/off lever (you'll find it next to the gas meter) by moving it so it is at right angles to the pipe. Open all doors and windows. Put out all naked lights and extinguish cigarettes with water. Do not turn any electrical switches either on or off as this can create a spark. Contact the Transco gas emergency number immediately (0800 111 999) if the smell of gas persists, and call a qualified gas fitter to trace the fault if it disperses.

**3** Keep the key to your gas meter box (above) somewhere safe and make sure that everyone knows where it is. The main on/off lever for your supply may be inside the box (which is usually at the front of the house) and you will need access to it quickly in an emergency.

**4** Always buy gas appliances that comply with British or European standards.

## GAS SAFETY REGULATIONS

The Gas Safety (Installation and Use) Regulations make it illegal for anyone to carry out work relating to gas supply and fittings who is not 'competent'. In practice, this means leaving all work on your gas supply system to a qualified gas fitter who is registered with CORGI (The Council for Registered Gas Installers).

**5** Have gas appliances serviced at least annually by a qualified CORGI-registered fitter. Look out for danger signs. If there is sooting round an appliance, if it burns with an orange or lazy flame, or if there is excessive condensation nearby, it may be faulty. Call the Transco gas emergency number and stop using it until it has been checked.

**6** Ensure that rooms containing gas-burning appliances are properly ventilated. If you get headaches or nausea when they are operating, they may be burning fuel unsafely and cr eating potentially lethal carbon monoxide (CO) gas. Ask your gas supplier for advice if you are concerned.

**7** For complete safety, have a gas detector installed – ideally a mains-powered one made to British Standard **BS EN 50194:2000** – look for the British Standards Kitemark (right). Also fit a carbon monoxide detector made to **BS 7860**. This is particularly important if you have gas heaters in bedrooms.

# What to do if you suspect a gas leak

The gas distribution company in your area will send an engineer, free of charge, if you smell gas. If the leak is inside your home, they may need to make it safe by turning off the supply until the fault has been repaired.

If you smell gas, first check whether a pilot light on a boiler, water heater, gas fire or cooker has gone out, or if a burner on the cooker has blown out in a draught or been extinguished by a pan boiling over. If any gas appliances are on, turn them off. If pilot lights are still on and all gas appliances are switched off, and there is still a smell, there may be a gas escape.

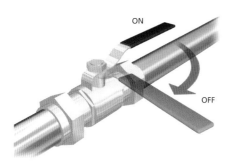

ON

OFF

**1** Turn off the main gas tap if you can get to it. This will be on the gas pipe adjacent to or near the gas meter. The meter is either indoors – usually in a kitchen or utility room – or in a meter cupboard outdoors. When the lever is at right angles to the pipe the gas is off.

**2** Don't turn any electric switches on or off or use doorbells or mobile phones.

**3** Don't smoke, light a match or use any other kind of naked flame.

**4** Open doors and windows to get rid of the gas.

**5** Get out of the house as quickly as possible.

**6** Call the Emergency Gas Service – **0800 111 999**. Once you are out of range of the gas it is safe to use a mobile phone; otherwise use a neighbour's telephone or a public callbox.

## What the engineer will do

A National Grid engineer will always 'make safe' when called to a suspected gas escape. However, under the terms of its licence, the National Grid will not repair appliances or installation pipework if the work cannot be completed within 30 minutes – so making safe usually means cutting off the gas supply to the appliance, and sometimes to your home.

**DO NOT USE!**

This Appliance must not be used until it is repaired and tested by a competent person. It is an offence to continue using an unsafe appliance.

**CONTACT A CORGI REGISTERED INSTALLER**
The Gas Safety (Installation & Use) Regulations 1998

**UNSAFE APPLIANCE**

## What you must do

The engineer will tell you what work needs to be done, and explain that this must be carried out by a CORGI registered engineer. He will not recommend an engineer – that is your responsibility. Look in your local Yellow Pages or call the free 24-hour repair helpline on 0800 371782 for the names and contact details of CORGI engineers in your area.

---

**WHAT THE EMERGENCY GAS SERVICE, 0800 111 999, WILL ASK YOU:**

- Your name, address and telephone number
- Where the smell of gas is most noticeable
- When the smell of gas was first noticed
- Whether the gas supply has been turned off
- Whether there is any smell of gas outside
- Whether there are any special instructions for access.

# Preventing accidents

Householders are responsible for ensuring that all the gas fittings and appliances in their home are safe to use. Gas appliances and flues should be regularly maintained and annual safety checks carried out by a CORGI-registered engineer.

Around thirty people a year are killed by carbon monoxide (CO) poisoning as a result of faulty gas appliances or blocked flues. Many others also suffer from headaches, lethargy or other symptoms but don't associate these with CO inhalation, but persistent headaches, especially if you always notice them in a particular room, can be a life-saving warning that an appliance is faulty. When gas does not burn properly, excess CO is produced. You cannot see, taste it or smell this poisonous gas, but CO can kill without warning in just a matter of hours.

## KEEPING SAFE WITH GAS

• Have domestic gas heating and hot water systems and appliances checked and serviced every year by a registered CORGI engineer (to find one go to www.corgi-gas.com).
• Fit a carbon monoxide detector.
• Note the position of your gas meter and mains valve and know how to turn off the gas in an emergency (see page 25).
• Ensure that the National Gas Emergency Service phone number 0800 111 999 is in a visible place.
• Make sure there is adequate ventilation in all rooms where there is a gas appliance.
• Do not cover ventilation grills or flues – they let waste gases escape.
• Have gas flues inspected regularly – they can get blocked by birds' nests, cobwebs and other debris.
• If you get a headache when a gas appliance is being used, check for carbon monoxide using a detector pad, available cheaply from DIY stores.

**Cookers** Keep gas hobs as clean as you can, removing any spilt food promptly before it burns on and becomes harder to clean. Gas jets, including the pilot light, can easily become blocked, so clear them from time-to-time with a matchstick or a piece of fine wire. If the flame burns blue (left) you know that a burner is working properly and burning the gas efficiently.

**Boilers and water heaters** Pilot lights can go out due to low gas pressure, allowing gas to escape. The pilot light going out could be caused by an accumulation of dust, dirt or grease around the jet. Again, these can be cleaned with a matchstick or a piece of fine wire.

**Gas fires** Unless your gas fire is designed to look like real coals burning in a grate, gas flames should always be blue. If the flame burns yellow or orange or if you begin to notice stains on the front grill or glass of your fire, it may not be working properly. Have the appliance checked promptly by a CORGI-registered gas fitter (see the box above for advice on how to find a appropriate engineer).

# Recovery position

The recovery position is a safe position in which to place an unconscious casualty. It protects from injury by stopping the victim from rolling over, and ensures that the airway stays open and fluids – blood, saliva or vomit – can drain away without risk of choking.

**2** Place the victim's other arm across the chest and support the cheek on the back of the hand. Bend the opposite knee upwards and pull to roll the victim towards you.

**1** **Call an ambulance immediately**. Kneel at the side of the victim, straighten the legs and place the arm nearest to you at a right angle to the body, with the forearm at a right angle to the upper arm.

**3** Support and protect the victim's head while rolling over. Keep the knee bent to prevent the victim from rolling too far.

**4** Tilt the victim's head back to keep the airway open, keeping it supported by the back of the victim's hand. Check pulse and breathing regularly until medical help arrives.

Tilt the chin back with one hand supporting the head, to keep the airway open and allow fluids to drain from the mouth.

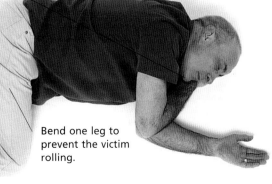

Bend one leg to prevent the victim rolling.

# Water safety

Although water itself is not dangerous, a major leak inside the house can do a great deal of damage. It can also cause an electrical short circuit if it penetrates any wiring.

Leaking water may come from one of four main sources: follow these guidelines to minimise the damage.

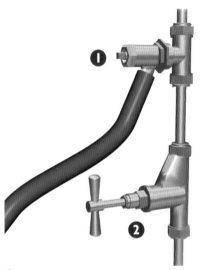

**1 The rising main stoptap** controls the flow of water into the house. It supplies the cold water storage tank, any feed-and-expansion tank, the kitchen cold tap and some appliances, such as a washing machine. Turning it off prevents tanks from refilling, and stems leaks from kitchen supply pipes. The rising main can be drained (above) via the drain valve ❶, which is usually near the stoptap ❷. Attach a length of garden hose to direct the water out of doors.

**2 The cold water storage tank** supplies all other cold taps in the house, and also the WC cisterns. There may be an on/off valve on the supply pipe leading from the tank. Turning it off and opening all cold taps will stop leaks from these pipes. If there is no valve, turn off the rising main stoptap and open all cold taps to drain the storage tank and stop the leak.

**3 The hot water storage cylinder** is supplied from the storage tank. If the cylinder or its supply pipe develops a leak, the cylinder must be drained using the drain valve close to its base. Attach a length of garden hose to direct the contents out of doors. Turn off the supply to the cylinder or empty the storage tank as described above. Opening hot taps will not drain the cylinder.

**4 The feed-and-expansion tank** tops up water losses from the heating system. If the heating system develops a leak, turn off the boiler and drain the system using the drain valve at the lowest point.

## WATER SUPPLY BYE-LAWS

Each water supply company has bye-laws to prevent waste or contamination of the water supply. The bye-laws require you to give your water supplier at least five working days' notice if you intend to install or alter a bidet, a flushing cistern, a tap to which a hose may be connected, or any other fitting which may allow used or stored water to be drawn back into the mains. You can get a copy of the bye-laws from your water supplier.

# Plumbing emergencies – what to do if:

## Water pours from the loft

**1** Turn the main stoptap off (clockwise). It is usually close to the kitchen sink. Put buckets under the leaks, then turn on all the cold taps in the house and flush all the WCs to drain the cold water storage cistern.

**2** Find the cause of the trouble. It may be a burst pipe in the loft or a cistern overflow caused by a blocked overflow pipe.

## No water comes from a tap

**1** If no water flows from the kitchen sink cold tap, check that the main stoptap is open. If it is, call your water supply company. You will find the number under 'Water' in the phone book.

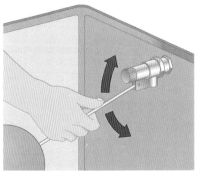

**2** If no water flows from other taps, check the cold water cistern. It may have emptied because of a jammed ballvalve.

If it is empty, move the float arm sharply up and down to free the valve, then clean the valve.

**Alternatively** In frosty weather there may be an ice plug blocking a supply pipe. If the kitchen cold tap is working, check the flow into the cold water cistern by pressing down the ballvalve. If there is no inflow, the rising main is frozen, probably between the ceiling and the cistern inlet.

**3** If the cistern is filling, check the taps in the bathroom. If there is no flow, the tap's supply pipe from the cistern is frozen.

**4** To thaw a pipe, strip off any lagging from the affected part and apply hot water bottles. If a pipe is difficult to get at, blow warm air onto it with a hairdryer.

**WARNING** Do not use a blowtorch to defrost a frozen pipe. It may cause a fire, or melt the solder in a pipe joint and cause another leak.

## Hot water cylinder leaks

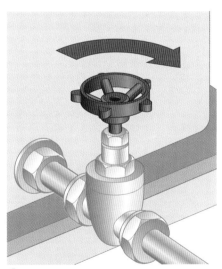

**1** Turn off the gatevalve (clockwise) on the supply pipe from the cold water cistern to the hot water cylinder. If there is no gatevalve, turn off the main stoptap and turn on all the taps to empty the cistern. (This will not empty the hot water cylinder, but will stop water from flowing into it.)

**2** Switch off immersion heater, if fitted.

**3** Switch off the boiler or put out the boiler fire.

**4** Connect a hose to the cylinder drain valve, which is located near the base of the cylinder where the supply pipe from the cold water cistern enters. Put the other end of the hose into an outside drain.

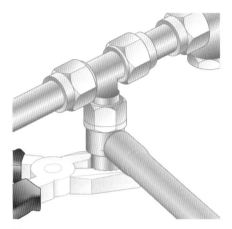

**5** Open up the drain valve with a drain valve key or pliers.

**6** Get the hot water cylinder repaired or replaced by a plumber.

## You cannot turn off the water

If you cannot turn off the water at the main stoptap, tie up the float arm in the cold water cistern to stop it filling, turn on all the taps (except the kitchen cold tap) and flush the WCs. You can then work on the problem pipe.

To work on the rising main, locate the outdoor stoptap (page 32). Use a stoptap key (available from plumbers' merchants) to turn off the tap and cut off the mains supply to the house.

## Other plumbing problems

## TRADE ORGANISATIONS

**Association of Plumbing and Heating Contractors**
Ensign House
Ensign Business Centre
Westwood Way
Coventry
CV4 8JA
Tel: 0800 542 6060
Fax: 024 7647 0626
Email: enquiries@aphc.co.uk

www.aphc.co.uk

**Institute of Plumbing**
64 Station Lane
Hornchurch
Essex
RM12 6NB
Tel: 01708 472791
Fax: 01708 448987
Email: info@plumbers.org.uk

www.plumbers.org.uk

**CORGI (Council for Registered Gas Installers)**
1 Elmwood
Chineham Park
Crockford Lane
Basingstoke
RG24 8WG
Tel: 0870 401 2200
Fax: 0870 401 2600
Email: enquiries@corgi-gas.com

www.corgi-gas-safety.com

# Cutting off the water supply

In a plumbing emergency, you will need to cut off the water supply. In many homes, only the kitchen tap is fed from the rising main; others are fed from the cold water cistern.

## Taps fed from the cistern

1 To isolate a hot or cold tap supplied from the cistern, turn off the gatevalve on the supply pipe from the cistern. If a service valve (see page 32) is fitted in the pipe to the tap, turn it off with a screwdriver.

2 Turn on the tap until the water has stopped flowing.

Alternatively If there is no gatevalve or service valve on the pipe, you will have to drain the cistern.

## Draining the cistern

1 Tie the ballvalve arm to a piece of wood laid across the cistern. This stops the flow into the cistern from the mains.

2 Turn on the bathroom cold taps until the water stops flowing, then turn on the hot taps – very little water will flow from them. (You need not turn off the boiler, as the hot water cylinder will not be drained.)

## Taps fed from the rising main

Turn off the main indoor stoptap, then turn on the mains-fed tap until the water stops.

Draining the rising main

You may want to drain the rising main to repair the main stoptap or to take a branch pipe from it to feed a new tap. If there is a drain valve above the stoptap, fit a short piece of hose to its outlet and open it with a drain valve key or pliers. Catch the water, usually only a litre or two, in a bucket.

### HELPFUL TIP

A stoptap that has been open for a long time may be jammed. To guard against this, close and open the stoptap fully twice a year. After opening it, give the handle a quarter turn towards closure. This prevents jamming without affecting water flow. If a stoptap is difficult to turn, apply a few drops of penetrating oil round the spindle base and leave for ten minutes before turning the handle again. Repeat as necessary.

# Turning off the outdoor stoptap

You may need to turn off the outdoor stoptap if the indoor one is broken, jammed or has a leak from the spindle. Stoptap keys can be bought from plumbers' merchants, but first check the type needed – the tap may have a crutch handle or a square spindle.

**Alternatively** If you have no stoptap key, make your own. Take a piece of strong wood about 1m long and in one end cut a V-shaped slot about 25mm wide at the opening and 75mm deep. Securely fix a piece of wood as a cross-bar handle at the other end. Slip the slot over the stoptap handle to turn it. This tool will not turn a stoptap with a square spindle.

**1** Locate the stoptap, which is under a cover, about 100mm across, just inside or just outside the boundary of your property. If you cannot find the outdoor stoptap, call your water supply company.

**2** Raise the cover. This may be difficult if it has not been raised for some time.

**3** Insert the stoptap key into the guard pipe and engage the stoptap handle at the bottom. Turn it clockwise.

# TYPES OF STOPTAP AND ISOLATING VALVE

**Stoptap** A tap with a valve and washer that is inserted into a mains-pressure supply pipe to control the water flow through it. A stoptap is usually kept turned on, being turned off only when necessary to cut off the supply. It must be fitted the right way round (an arrow mark shows the flow direction). Most stoptaps have a crutch handle.

**Drain valve** A tap without a handle, opened by turning the spindle with a drain valve key. It is normally kept closed, but has a ribbed outlet for attaching a hose when draining is necessary. A drain valve is fitted in those parts of the plumbing system that cannot be drained through household taps – for instance, in the boiler or central-heating systems and on the rising main.

**Gatevalve** An isolating valve with a wheel handle, through which the water flow is controlled by raising or lowering a metal plate (or gate). It can be fitted either way round and is normally used in low-pressure pipes such as supply pipes from a storage cistern. With the gate open, the flow is completely unrestricted. When it is closed, the seal is not as watertight as a stoptap.

**Service valve** A small isolating valve operated with a screwdriver. This turns a pierced plug inside the valve to stop or restore the water flow. Normally used in a low-pressure supply pipe to a tap or ballvalve to cut off the water for repairs. A similar valve with a small lever handle and a threaded outlet is used to control the flow to the flexible supply hoses of a washing machine or dishwasher.

# Repairing a burst pipe

Metal pipes are more likely to suffer frost damage than plastic pipes. Copper and stainless steel pipes are less vulnerable than softer lead pipes.

As an ice plug forms, it expands and may split the pipe or force open a joint. When the ice melts, the pipe or fitting leaks. A split copper or plastic pipe can be temporarily repaired with a proprietary burst-pipe repair clamp. In an emergency, a pipe not under mains pressure can be patched with a length of garden hose.

Make a permanent repair as soon as possible. Cut off the water supply (page 31), drain the pipe and replace the damaged length. For a split less than 90mm long in a copper pipe, you can make a permanent repair with a slip coupling.

For lead piping, use a tape-repair kit for a strong repair that will allow you to restore the water supply until a plumber can make a permanent repair (working on lead pipework is best left to a professional).

## EMERGENCY PIPE REPAIRS

To make a permanent, conventional repair to a burst or leaking pipe, you need to turn off the water supply and potentially drain down the entire system. An emergency alternative is to use a DIY pipe freezing kit. This includes a carbon dioxide aerosol spray and a 'freezer jacket' that wraps around the affected pipe ahead of the leak and freezes the water inside to create a plug to stop the flow. The kit will keep the pipe frozen for around 35 minutes – just long enough for a quick repair or a temporary fix to be put in place.

## Patching a split branch pipe

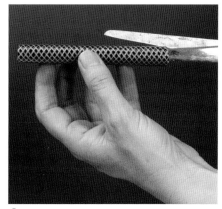

**1** Cut a piece of garden hose that is long enough to cover the pipe for at least 50mm beyond the area of damage. Split the hose along its length.

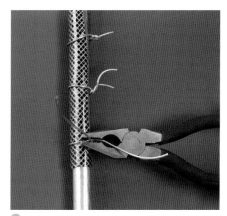

**2** Wrap the hose round the pipe to cover the damage and secure it with three loops of strong wire. Twist the loops closed tightly with pliers.

**Alternatively** Fit an emergency pipe repair clamp and tighten the screws fully with a screwdriver.

# Dealing with a blocked sink

A blocked sink may not pose any danger, but it's very inconvenient. Grease may have built up in the trap and waste pipe trapping food particles and other debris, or an object may be obstructing the waste pipe.

Tools *Possibly a length of wire; sink-waste plunger; sink auger or a length of expanding curtain wire; bucket.*

## Sink completely blocked

**1** If the water will not run away at all, place the sink plunger cup squarely over the plug hole.

**2** Stuff a damp cloth firmly into the overflow opening and hold it there. This stops air escaping through the hole and dissipating the force you build up by plunging. Pump the plunger sharply up and down. If the blockage does not clear, repeat the operation.

**3** If plunging fails, replace the sink plug. Put a bucket under the sink and disconnect the trap. Wash it out thoroughly if it is blocked with debris.

**4** If the obstruction is not in the trap, try using a plumber's snake. It is a spiral device that can be hired or bought. Disconnect the blocked pipe from its trap and feed the wire into it. Then turn the handle to rotate the spiral. This drives its cutting head into the blockage and breaks it up.

Alternatively If you have poured fat into the sink and it has hardened, try warming the pipe with a hair dryer, to melt the grease. Flush plenty of hot water after it.

# Clearing a blocked WC

The usual faults with a WC pan are blockages or leaks. A leak from the pan outlet is not difficult to repair.

## Clearing a washdown pan

If the flush water rises almost to the pan rim, then ebbs away very slowly, there is probably a blockage in the pan outlet (or possibly in the soil stack or drain into which it discharges).

Tools *WC plunger. Possibly also flexible drain auger; bucket; a pair of rubber gloves.*

**1** To clear the pan, take the plunger and push it sharply onto the bottom of the pan to cover the outlet. Then pump the handle up and down two or three times.

Alternatively If you have no WC plunger, you may be able to use a mop. Or stand on a stool and, all in one go, tip in a bucket of warm water.

**2** If this does not clear the pan, probe the outlet and trap with a flexible drain auger.

**3** If the blockage persists, check and clear the underground drain.

## Clearing a siphonic pan

Blockages are more common in siphonic pans because of the double trap and the delicate pressure reducing pipe seal. Do not use a plunger on a blocked siphonic pan because this can dislodge the seal.

A blockage can usually be cleared with an auger or by pouring several buckets of warm water into the pan.
As you insert the auger, turn it slowly. If you meet hard resistance turn the auger back and forth to move it past the trap. When you meet soft resistance, push and pull gently to dislodge the blockage. Finally, flush the bowl with a bucket of water.

## Repairing a leaking pan outlet

A putty joint may leak when the putty gets old and cracked.

To replace a putty joint with a push-fit connector, the pan must be moved forward then refitted. Alternatively, you can repair the joint using waterproof building tape or non-setting mastic filler.

Chip and rake out the old putty with an old chisel and bind two or three turns of tape round the pan outlet. Then poke more tape firmly into the rim of the soil-pipe inlet. Fill the space between the rim and pan outlet with mastic. Bind two more turns of tape round the joint.

# Choosing pipe insulation material

Insulating pipes is critical to prevent them from freezing and bursting in very cold weather, and to minimise heat lost as hot water travels around the system.

**Self-adhesive foam wrap** Thin foam insulating wrap, 50mm wide, is supplied in rolls usually 5m or 10m long. Some types have a metallic finish.

There is no formula for estimating how much wrap to buy – it depends on the size of the pipes and how large you make the overlaps. Buy and use one or two packs, then work out how much more you will need to complete the job.

Before you fix the lagging, make sure that the pipes are clean and dry. Peel off the backing paper and wind the material round the pipes. Overlap the tape as you wind, especially at bends. This flexible lagging is also useful for insulating awkward fittings, such as stoptaps.

## COLD-WEATHER CHECKS

• Make sure no tap is left dripping. If that is not possible, put a plug in the bath or basin overnight. Drips cause ice to block waste pipes.

• Never allow cisterns to overfill. Water in overflow pipes can freeze, causing the cistern to overspill.

• In a long cold spell, open the loft hatch occasionally, to let in warmth from the house.

• If you leave the house for short periods, keep the central heating switched on, but turned down to the minimum setting.

• For long periods, drain the plumbing system by closing the main stoptap and opening all the taps. When the water stops running, open the drain valve near the stoptap.

**Plastic foam tubes** Easy-to-fit plastic foam tubes are split down one side and have to be eased open to fit them round the pipe. They are secured with adhesive tape wrapped round at intervals, or with purpose-made clips. Tubes are available to fit 15mm, 22mm and 28mm pipes. Plastic foam tube is slightly more expensive than self-adhesive foam wrap, but is easier to fit. Foam tubes are available in two wall thicknesses. In most cases the standard grade is sufficient, but
if you live in an area that often experiences severe frosts or if your pipes are particularly exposed, it is worth investing in the thicker material.

**Glass fibre blanket** Pipes that are boxed in can be insulated by stuffing glass fibre blanket around the pipes.

**Cut neat joints** Make 45° cuts in split-sleeve foam tubes with scissors or a serrated knife so you can form neat joins at elbows and tees. Use PVC insulating tape to keep the joints tightly closed and avoid a freeze-up.

# Insulating hot and cold water pipes

Hot and cold water pipes that are exposed to the cold should be lagged to prevent winter freeze-ups.

**Before you start** Concentrate first on pipes that run across a loft, above an insulated floor, and those that run along outside walls in unheated rooms. Overflow and vent pipes that are exposed to the cold should also be lagged. Some pipes are boxed in. To lag them, unscrew the box and stuff pieces of glass fibre insulation all round the pipes. Make sure all pipes are clean and dry before you start.

## Lagging pipes with self-adhesive foam wrap

**Tools** *Scissors.*

**Materials** *Rolls of self-adhesive foam wrap.*

Self-adhesive foam wrap is useful where there are many bends in the pipes and it would be difficult to use flexible foam tubes.

**1** For pipes in the loft, begin work at the cistern. Cut pieces of foam wrap to a workable length with scissors.

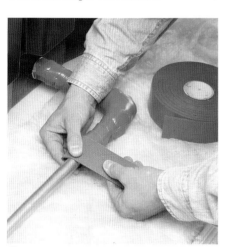

**2** Wrap foam round the pipe, making generous overlaps of about one-third of the width of the wrap. Take care to cover the pipe well at bends – these are the vulnerable areas most likely to freeze.

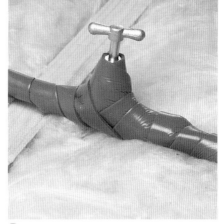

**3** Take the wrap around any valves or stoptaps as you meet them, leaving only the handle exposed.

## Lagging pipes with flexible foam tube

**Tools** *Scissors; serrated knife.*

**Materials** *Foam tube to match pipe size; adhesive tape; plastic clips.*

**1** Lag the pipes leading from the cistern first, if you are insulating pipes in the loft. Wrap plastic adhesive tape around the first tube to hold it in place, even if the tube is one of the self-locking types. Push it up tight against the cistern so that the tank connector joint is covered.

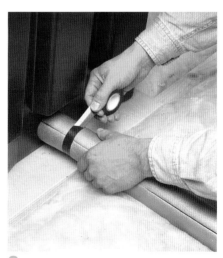

**2** Butt-join the tubes where they meet and wrap round the join to hold them tight. Cut the tube at 45° to fit it round elbows and tee fittings, and tape the joints. Alternatively secure joints with plastic clips.

**3** Cut the tube to fit round the body of a gatevalve as closely as possible.

# Lagging a cold water cistern

Never lay lagging under a cold water cistern. Heat rising through the ceiling will help to prevent a freeze-up.

Before you start Purpose-made jackets are available to insulate most cisterns. Measure the cistern's diameter and height, if it is round, and its height, length and width if it is rectangular.

It does not matter if the jacket you buy is too large, since the sections can be overlapped. If the cistern is an odd size or shape, or you want to provide extra insulation, use plastic-sleeved glass fibre loft insulation blanket. This is easier to handle than unsleeved blanket and will not release fibres into the air as you handle it.

## Using glass fibre blanket

Tools *Steel tape measure; scissors.*

Materials *150mm thick wrapped glass fibre blanket; string.*

1 Wrap the cistern in a continuous length of blanket, which you have cut with scissors so that the edges will meet. Tie a length of string round the blanket.

2 If necessary, wrap a second length of blanket round the tank. Cut it to length and tie it on the same way as the first layer.

3 Extend the top layer beyond the top of the tank, to create a small rim to hold the tank's lid in place.

4 Measure the size of the tank lid. Cut a length of blanket to match and staple the ends closed. If the blanket is too wide, squeeze it up tightly to fit. Do not cut the blanket along its length.

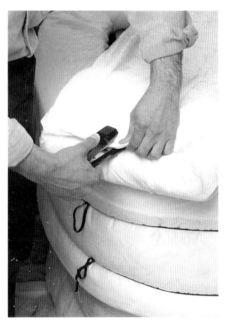

# Leaks in a central heating system

Never ignore leaks in a central heating system. Fresh water that is drawn in to replace the lost water contains free oxygen which can cause radiators and cast iron boilers to rust.

**Before you start** Internal leak sealants similar to the radiator 'weld' used in cars can be used to seal very minor leaks. Pour the sealant in through the feed-and-expansion tank. You cannot use leak sealant in a sealed system.

## A leaking pipe joint

Most leaking pipe joints are compression fittings, which can be tightened with a spanner. Tighten the joint slightly, no more than a quarter turn. If this does not stop the leak, do not tighten any further as this will damage the joint.

**1** Drain the system to below the level of the leak. Undo the nut on the leaking joint and pull the pipe out slightly.

**2** Wrap two or three turns of PTFE tape around the face of the olive where it meets the joint. Tighten the nut.

**3** If the leaking joint is soldered, drain the system. Heat the joint with a blowtorch and take it apart, then replace it.

## A leaking radiator valve

If the leak is from the compression joint below the valve, drain down the system to below the joint. Then call a plumber or repair the joint yourself.
   Use PTFE tape to cure a leak from the union nut connecting the valve to the radiator.

**1** Turn off the valves at both ends of the radiator, counting the number of turns taken to close the lockshield valve. Write the number down.

**2** Put a towel and a bowl under the valve to catch water, and have a bucket and a second bowl ready.

**3** Use an adjustable spanner to turn the union nut counter-clockwise (when looking from the radiator to the valve). Some water may run out.

**4** Open the air vent to allow the rest of the water to flow out. Collect it in containers.

**5** Wind PTFE tape tightly around the male thread on the valve tail. Start at the end and make a 50 per cent overlap on each turn.

**6** Screw the nut back on, and open the valves and air vent. Open the lockshield valve by the number of turns that were necessary to close it. Check for leaks and close the air vent when water flows from it.

## A leaking valve tail

The leak may be from the valve tail screwed into the radiator. Use a radiator spanner to remove it. Cover the male thread on the valve tail with PTFE tape and replace the tail.

## A leaking radiator vent

If the radiator air vent leaks, drain the system to below the vent. Remove the air-vent fitting using a radiator spanner. Bind the screw joint with PTFE tape, and replace the fitting.

## A leaking radiator

A small jet of water from the body of the radiator is called a pinhole leak. It is caused by internal corrosion and can happen within a few weeks of the system being fitted if the debris that collects during installation has not been removed, or if air is being drawn in.

Turn off the valves at each end to relieve the pressure. Then remove the radiator and leave the rest of the system running. Before fitting a new radiator, flush out and clean the system using a non-acidic cleaner.

## Repacking a radiator gland

If a radiator valve weeps water from under the cap, the packing gland is worn. You can replace the packing with PTFE tape or thread-sealing fibre, sold by plumbers' merchants. 'Belmont' radiator valves cannot be repacked; instead they have renewable O-rings which can be replaced with a kit.

Tools *Small adjustable spanner; small screwdriver; PTFE tape; silicone grease.*

**1** Turn off the handwheel valve. If it continues to leak, close the lockshield valve at the other end of the radiator.

**2** Remove the cap from the leaking valve and use an adjustable spanner to undo the small gland nut. Slide it up out of the way.

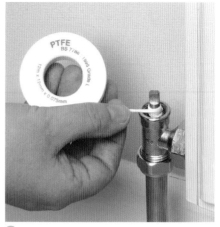

**3** Slide the nut up out of the way. Pull a length of PTFE tape into a string and wrap this around the spindle four or five times.

**4** Use a small screwdriver to push the tape down into the valve body.

**5** Smear on silicone grease and re-tighten the gland nut. Replace the head and turn the valve back on.

# Protect your home from fire

There are nearly 70,000 fires in people's homes each year, resulting in over 400 deaths and around 14,000 injuries. Fires can start easily and spread with terrifying speed. It is essential that you know how to tackle them effectively and quickly, and have a plan for getting everyone out safely.

Nearly 20 people a day are killed in house fires, therefore it is vital to be alert to the dangers of fire. The first thing to remember if a fire does start in your home is that, however small it is, get everyone out of the building and then dial 999 for the Fire and Rescue Service.

A fire can be caused by an electrical fault, by careless use of tools that generate heat – such as a blowlamp or heat gun – or by incorrect use or storage of flammable materials. For general household protection, fit a smoke detector (see page 42) made to British Standard BS 5446-1:2000 on each floor of the house, and change the batteries every year to ensure that the detectors are always in full working order. Keep a fire blanket in the kitchen and an all-purpose fire extinguisher in the workshop.

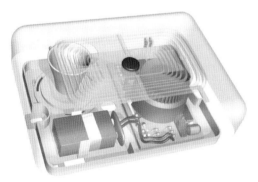

## SMOKE ALARMS

Building Regulations require mains-powered smoke alarms to be fitted in new properties and existing homes that are extended or where the loft has been converted. The Home Office recommends that at least two alarms approved to British Standard BS5446 Part 1 are fitted in an average two-storey house – one downstairs in the hall and the other on the landing.

Smoke alarms should be fitted within 7.5m of the door to every habitable room – living rooms, kitchens and bedrooms. An alarm fitted to the ceiling should be at least 300mm away from a wall or ceiling light fitting. If fitted to the wall, it must be between 150mm and 300mm below the ceiling.

Smoke alarms for existing homes can be battery-operated, wired to the mains with a back-up battery or plugged into a ceiling light fitting (above).

There are two basic types: ionisation and photoelectric (optical). For good, all-round protection use one of each. The ionisation alarm works by detecting invisible smoke particles in the air, while the photoelectric alarm 'sees' smoke and is therefore more sensitive to smouldering fires.

Both types run off nine-volt batteries, which you should test every week. There are also alarms available with ten-year batteries, which cost a bit more but you do save on the annual charge for replacement batteries. They are fitted with a long-life lithium battery or a sealed power pack.

Some battery-powered alarms have indicators to show that the battery is still working; others give an audible warning when the battery is low. Plug-in alarms recharge when the light is switched on. Accumulated dust impairs performance, so clean alarms regularly using a vacuum cleaner nozzle.

### SAFETY TIP

Of the 460 people killed in house fires each year, on average:
• 270 of the 460 people didn't have a smoke alarm;
• 90 of them had a smoke alarm that didn't work, usually because the battery was flat or missing.

# The best alarm for the job

In the UK in 2004, more than 285,000 fire call-outs were false alarms caused by fire detectors. Responding to false alarms wastes valuable fire service time, so make sure that you choose an appropriate smoke detector for your situation.

Fire alarms detect fire risk using various methods. The best way to avoid false alarms is to choose the right detector for the job. If it goes off when you are cooking or have just lit the fire, you may have picked the wrong type of detector or sited it in the wrong place. Persistent false alarms are irritating and it may be tempting to remove the battery and disable the alarm (below). Never do this. Instead, reposition the alarm away from the source of the bathroom steam or cooking fumes that set it off or replace it with a different model.

**Ionisation smoke detectors** quickly detect fast-burning fires that produce small smoke particles, and that can burn for some time without generating much smoke. These are the best general-purpose detectors.

**Optical smoke detectors** are a general smoke alarm particularly suitable for slow, smouldering fires such as soft furnishing fires, which produce smoke with large particles. They are good for bedrooms, living rooms and hallways.

**Heat detectors** cut down on false alarms in smoky or dusty areas, such as kitchens and garages, where there may be high levels of steam and other airborne particles that trigger smoke alarms. These 'rate-of-rise'

## CEILING ROSE ALARM

A combined smoke alarm and emergency light is available as a ceiling rose fitting. It is powered by the lighting circuit but it also has a back-up battery, which recharges itself when the light is on. The alarm incorporates an emergency light, which activates automatically when mains power fails. Several units can be linked in a series, so that in the event of fire the alarms are activated throughout the house, providing an illuminated escape route.

Other types of smoke alarm can also be wired into the lighting circuit. It is worth considering an interconnecting system. Then, if an alarm is triggered downstairs, for example, the upstairs alarms go off, too, giving people in the bedrooms plenty of time to escape.

heat detectors react to a rapid increase in temperature, so they respond only when a fire is well established and generating a lot of heat.

**Smoke alarms for the deaf** provide three warning signals – visual and vibrating as well as audio – for the hard of hearing.

**Radio interlinked smoke and heat alarms** link several alarms through radio waves – if one alarm detects fire, all alarms sound.

## The future of fire alarms

A fire detector that can tell the difference between burning bacon or the steam from a hot shower and a smouldering mattress sounds too good to be true – but one is currently being developed for domestic use. The detector uses several sensors and a 'neural network' to determine whether the heat or smoke it's detecting are from a fire or just part of a room's environment.

Most home alarms go off when smoke particles in the air exceed a certain concentration. But the new detector has both thermal sensors, to monitor temperature and its rate of change, and optical sensors to monitor smoke. Each detector is programmed on installation to reflect normal circumstances in that room. So a detector on the landing outside the bathroom will be programmed to ignore steam but to react to smoke particles or an unusually high temperature.

# Putting out a fire

A fire extinguisher is a cylinder containing a pressurised substance that shoots out in a jet. There are three main types: water, foam and powder. If you use the wrong one, you will make the fire worse.

If you decide to buy a fire extinguisher, choose one filled either with multi-purpose dry powder or aqueous film forming foam (AFFF). Both work well on many types of common domestic fires and are the safest choices for home use.

**A multi-purpose powder extinguisher** knocks down the flames and, on burning solids, melts to form a skin smothering the fire. Do not use on chip-pan fires as the

## KEEP EQUIPMENT TO HAND

A fire blanket or extinguisher should be easy to reach in an emergency. Never hide equipment in a cupboard or mount it above a cooker or heater: you may find that you cannot get to it in the event of fire. Keep a fire blanket in the kitchen, where it is most likely to be needed. If you have a fire extinguisher, keep it in the hall, where it can be fetched quickly from any other room in the house. If you have a garage or workshop, keep another fire extinguisher there, too.

powerful jet could spread the burning oil. Aim the jet at the base of the flames and sweep it briskly from side to side.

**An AFFF foam extinguisher** will put out most fires but must not be used on electrical fires – as the foam could conduct electricity back to you – nor chip-pan fires as the foam could spread the burning oil. If a solid object is on fire, aim the jet at the base of the flames and move it over the area of the fire. If a liquid is burning, aim the foam at a nearby vertical surface, not straight at the fire; allow the foam to build up and flow across the burning liquid.

**Water-filled extinguishers** are suitable only on solid materials, such as burning paper or wood. If you use water on electrical fires, you risk an electric shock, while oil fires can explode as water hits them. Water-filled types are generally not recommended for home use.

## Fire blankets

Fire blankets work well on fat pan fires and can also be used to wrap around someone whose clothing is on fire. Always keep one in the kitchen, close to the cooker but not directly above the hob, where you may not be able to reach it safely in the event of a pan fire on the stove top.

A fire blanket is a fire resistant sheet of material. When placed over a fire it cuts its oxygen supply, putting it out. It is light, and quick and easy to use. The main disadvantage of a fire blanket is that you must be very close to the fire in order to use it and could easily burn your hands as you throw the blanket over the flames. A fire blanket is suitable only for small fires that will be contained within the area of the open blanket.

## How to use a fire blanket

• Pull tapes to remove the blanket from its case – and check that the fire is smaller than the blanket.
• Hold the blanket well up in front of you by the tapes, keeping your hands tucked behind it.
• Cover the fire with the blanket to smother it. Leave the blanket in place for at least 30 minutes.

# Fire in the kitchen

More than half of all accidental fires in the home start in the kitchen, most involving the cooker. If a fire is small and contained, fast action can stop it from spreading. However, if fire has taken hold, get everyone out fast.

On average, there are still 16,000 chip-pan fires each year in the UK. These damage homes, cause around 3,000 injuries and kill some 30 people.

Chip-pan fires start when the oil overheats and catches fire, or when oil spills onto the hob because the pan has been overfilled. They can also start when you lower wet chips into hot oil, causing it to bubble up and overflow.

## If a chip pan or frying pan catches fire

If a chip pan or frying pan catches fire, don't panic and don't move the pan.
• **Turn off the heat** if it's safe to do so, but never lean over the pan to reach the controls.
• **Cover the pan** with a fire blanket or a damp towel.

## FIRE EXTINGUISHER GUIDELINES

• Only use for fighting a fire in its very early stages.
• Never use on a chip-pan fire.
• Have it serviced properly once a year.
• Site where you can reach it quickly and safely.
• Buy one you can carry easily.
• Read the instructions so you know how to use it – don't wait until you have a fire.
• When using it, stay on the escape-route side of the fire.

• **Leave the pan to cool down** for at least half an hour, even if the flames seem to have died down. The addition of oxygen will reignite the flames.

Unless the fire is small and contained within the pan, you will not be able to control it. Close the door to the room, get out and tell everybody else to get out, too. **Call the fire brigade – 999** – and do not go back inside for any reason.

## Fry food safely

The best safety advice you could take regarding your chip pan would be to throw it away and buy a thermostatically controlled deep-fat fryer – or use oven chips. If you are wedded to your chip pan, then follow these safety rules:
• Never fill the pan more than a third full with oil.
• Never leave a pan unattended with the heat on – even for a few seconds.
• Dry chips before putting them in the pan.
• Never put food into a pan if the oil has started smoking or it could ignite – turn off the heat and let the oil cool down.

## FAT OR OIL PAN FIRES

• NEVER use an extinguisher on a fat or oil pan fire.
• NEVER throw water onto a fat or oil pan fire.

# Electrical fire

It only takes one old or badly wired plug to start a fire. The wires do not even need to touch for a spark to jump and a fire to start.

If there is a fire in your home, the first consideration, always, is people's safety. This applies to electrical fires, too.
• **Don't take risks** Get everyone out and dial 999 for the fire brigade.
• **Cut the power** Pull the plug out or switch off the power at the fuse box. This may stop the fire immediately.
• **Don't touch** If an appliance is burning, do not touch the switch.
• **Never use water on electrical fires.**
• **Extinguish the flames** If you have a multi-purpose powder extinguisher, then aim the jet at the base of the flames and briskly sweep it from side to side. Don't use a water- or foam-filled extinguisher.
• **Smother the fire** If a TV or computer is burning, pull out the plug or switch off at the fuse box. Then smother the fire with a blanket, rug or, ideally, a fire blanket.

## PREVENTING ELECTRICAL FIRES

A few simple rules can help you to prevent electrical equipment from starting fires in your home.

• Turn off and unplug electrical appliances when you are not using them, unless the item is meant to be left switched on – a tuner with a date-and-time display, for example.
• Make sure each electrical appliance is fitted with the correct fuse. Use a 3amp fuse for equipment up to 700 watts, a 5amp fuse for appliances that use 700–1000 watts and a 13amp fuse for equipment over 1000 watts.
• Avoid multi-way block adaptors and never plug one adaptor into another. Overloading a socket can cause overheating and fire.
• Don't run extension leads or cables under carpets. If they wear through, no one will know.
• If a power lead has a crack or a hole in it, stop using it. Never mend a lead with insulating tape.

## Warning signs

If you have even the slightest worry about your electrics, call a qualified electrician. Do not attempt DIY electrical work if you are unsure. The following are all danger signs of problem wiring:
• Flickering lights
• Hot plugs and sockets
• Brown scorch marks on sockets and plugs
• Fuses blowing for no reason.

## Electric heaters

Electric heaters should be treated with respect. Buy heaters only from a reputable retailer. Use a fireguard with a radiant fire, especially if you have children, and sit at least one metre (3ft) away. Keep heaters clear of curtains and furniture and don't dry washing on or near them. Never cover the air grilles of storage heaters, fan heaters or convection heaters.

## Electric blankets

Electric blankets cause more than 250 fires a year. To protect the wiring, they should be stored flat or rolled up, never folded. They should not be switched on all night, unless thermostatically controlled for all-night use. It is important to check the blanket and its flex regularly. Look out for the following danger signs and, if in doubt, throw it out:
• Fraying fabric;
• Scorch marks;
• Exposed elements;
• Creasing or folding;
• Tie tapes damaged or missing;
• Worn flex or loose connections;
• Round British Electrotechnical Approvals Board (BEAB) safety symbol (right), which indicates that the blanket is more than ten years old. Newer blankets will carry the new BEAB mark for electrical goods (below right) or a version with white capital letters on a black background.

# Furniture and clothing fires

By law, all upholstered furniture, including second-hand items, must meet fire resistance standards. Check your furniture, as items made before 1988, or bought from an unreliable supplier, could be unsafe.

The fire safety regulations were introduced in 1988 because many types of foam, when they catch fire, give off lethal fumes that can kill in minutes. Upholstered furniture made since 1988 should have a stitched-on label detailing its fire resistance. Check your furniture. Look for the label and, if in doubt, contact your local fire service for further advice.

Fire resistant does not mean fireproof. If you smoke, never leave a lighted cigarette or pipe unattended – if it fell into an armchair or onto a carpet it could start a fire. Never smoke if you think you may doze off – smoking stretched out on a sofa or in bed is a major cause of fire.

## If furniture catches fire

The choking smoke from burning foam can kill in one minute. Do not try to put out the fire. Get out of the room and close the door to stop the smoke from spreading. Make sure everyone is safely out of the building, then dial 999.

## If clothing catches fire

If your clothing, or someone else's, catches fire, remember the drill:
• **Keep still** Don't let the victim run around in a panic. The movement will fan the flames and make them burn faster.
• **Lie down** This makes it harder for the fire to spread. It also reduces the effect of flames on the face and head – flames burn upwards.
• **Smother the flames** Wrap the victim tightly with heavy material, such as a coat, a blanket, curtains or a fire blanket. This will cut off the fire's supply of oxygen.
• **Douse the fire** If there is nothing suitable in which to wrap the victim, douse the flames with water or another non-flammable liquid – in a kitchen, a bottle of milk may be closest to hand.
• **Roll the victim around** Rolling also helps to smother the flames.
• Once the flames are out, cover the victim with a thin blanket or sheet to stop him or her from becoming cold.

### TAKE CARE WITH CANDLES

Always use candles or tea lights in a proper holder. Stand them on a flat, heat-resistant surface – never on top of a television and never close to curtains or in a draught. Keep candles out of reach of children and pets.

Always make sure that candles are properly extinguished, taking care to keep your hair and clothes away from the flames.

# A smell of burning or an alarm going off

**Have you thought about what you would do if your smoke alarm went off or you smelt burning?**

It only takes a careless moment for a fire to start. A couple of minutes later and your home might be filled with deadly smoke and fumes. You will have only a short time to get everyone out. Try to keep calm.

If you smell burning alert everyone in your home. If you think the fire has taken hold in a closed room, do not open the door – unless you are letting someone out – or the flames will spread.

Don't put yourself at risk unless you are sure that you can extinguish a fire. Dial 999 and ask for the Fire Brigade. If the fire is serious, leave the building before you make the phone call.

## DON'T GO BACK INSIDE

Never go back into a burning house to rescue a pet that you think may have been left behind. A dog's sense of smell is many times more sensitive than a person's and this keen sense of smell means they are often the first to know and to escape when there's smoke in the air.

## ESCAPE LADDERS

To escape from upstairs rooms, particularly loft conversions, it is worth considering fitting a specially designed escape ladder.

When not in use, some ladders fit into a small box, fixed to the wall beneath the windowsill – and these are simple enough for a child to use. You pull the cover towards you and throw the unit out of the window – the weight of the cover extends the ladder. Once the ladder has been

used, it must be sent back to the manufacturer for repacking. Ladders are available for buildings up to five storeys high. A ladder long enough to reach the ground from a dormer window costs approximately £115.

You can also buy various types of portable fire escape ladders that simply hook over a windowsill (below). Buy one with the right sized hook for your wall thickness and make sure everyone knows where it is kept and how to use it.

# Escaping a fire

Fires can start suddenly and spread quickly. An escape plan that the whole household is familiar with can save time – and lives

## If a fire starts

Try not to panic – tell everyone to get out and stay out and call the fire brigade. If possible, shut the door of the room where the fire is and shut all doors behind you as you leave. This will help to slow the spread of fire and smoke. Don't waste time trying to take anything with you.

Never open a door unless you have to escape through it. If you have to open a door, use the back of your hand to touch it first. If it feels warm, do not open it. The fire will be on the other side.

### WINDOW AND DOOR KEYS

What would you do if you were trapped in a first-floor bedroom and the window was locked – and the key was hanging on a hook in the understairs cupboard?

Always keep the key to unlock a window (below) in the same room as the window, but not in the lock, where a burglar could break the glass and use the key to open it.

For security, good advice is to lock the front door with more than just the cylinder latch overnight. But fumbling for a mortise lock key could cost valuable time in an emergency. A good solution is to fit rack bolts operated by a fixed thumb screw, not a key.

If you can't get out, get everyone into one room and shut the door – it is best if the room you retreat to has a window and a phone. Use towels, sheets or clothes to block gaps under the door to help stop the smoke from seeping into the room. Go to the window and shout to attract attention. Ask people to call the fire brigade.

If the room begins to get smoky stay by the window and lean out of it to breathe if you need to. If the window won't open, lie down on the floor – it will be easier to breathe there because smoke rises.

If you are on the first floor and in danger, do not jump. Drop cushions or bedding to the ground first to break your fall. Get out of the window feet first and lower yourself as far as you can before you let go. Check all windows in your house regularly to ensure that they open easily.

## Breaking a window

If you need to smash a window to get out, hit the bottom corner of the glass with a sharp object. Remove the loose glass and cover any remaining glass with bedding or clothing before climbing through.

## Always be alert

Discuss with your household regularly what to do and what not to do in a fire. Remind everyone where you keep keys for doors and windows. Work out the order you would escape in, so you can help others less able. Keep a reminder of what to do in a fire somewhere prominent.

## If you live in a high-rise flat

High-rise flats are built to be fireproof. Walls, ceilings and doors will hold back flames and smoke for quite a time.
• If there is a fire elsewhere in the building, don't investigate the fire. Stay in your flat unless heat or smoke are affecting you.
• If you need to leave for your own safety, get everyone in your home out with you and alert neighbouring flats by banging on their doors on your way out. Set off the fire alarm if there is one.
• If there is a lot of smoke, crawl along the floor where the air is clearer.
• Before you open any door check it with the back of your hand.
• Never use a lift if there is a fire – walk down the stairs.

## Children need to know what to do

It is important to talk through with children what to do in the event of a fire. There will be no time to stop and think if they are caught up in one. Don't avoid the subject for fear of giving them nightmares or frightening them. Children must know how to react to a fire as they may not have an adult with them when one starts to tell them what to do. It is important, just like adults, that they stay calm. They could even end up saving your life if they react swiftly and sensibly. So when you are making your escape plan, include everyone who lives in your home.

Write out this list of what to do (below). You can customise it for your own children and with instructions specific to your own house. Encourage them to illustrate it or to write it out themselves then stick it to the fridge or on the wall. This will help them to remember what to do in an emergency.

### 999 – HOW TO MAKE THAT LIFE-SAVING CALL

Once you have escaped, use a mobile, a neighbour's phone or a phone box – 999 calls are free. The more information the Fire and Rescue Service has, the quicker it can get to you and act when it gets there. Use the following guidelines:
• Speak slowly and clearly.
• Give your full address.
• State what type of home is on fire – for example, a second-floor flat or a two-storey house.
• Tell the operator if anyone is trapped and what room they are in.

# What to do if there's a fire

• If you see smoke or flames, or hear an alarm going off, tell a grown-up straight away if you can and wake people up if they are asleep.

• Get out of the building fast.

• Find a phone and call 999 - you may need to go next door to find a phone.

• Say there is a fire and when they ask for your address, say it slowly.

• Don't go back into the building for toys or pets.

• If there is lots of smoke, crawl along the floor as the air is less smoky there.

• If you can't get out, go into a room with a window, shut the door and put things like your clothes or pillows and duvets round the door to stop smoke getting in.

• Open the window and shout for help.

• Never hide in a cupboard or under a bed - no one will be cross with you.

# Burns and scalds

The most painful heat-related injuries are not always the most serious, so it is essential to treat them correctly and seek medical help quickly.

## WHAT TO LOOK FOR

- Severe pain or no pain
- Cold, clammy skin
- Nausea or vomiting
- Black or red skin which may be blistered
- Swelling
- Clear fluid weeping from the skin

Burns are caused by contact with a heat source, such as hot metal, or by corrosive chemicals, friction, radiation or electricity. Scalds are caused by steam or hot liquid. The amount of pain felt is not a true guide to the severity of the injury. Superficial and partial-thickness burns (involving only the skin) have a tendency to be more painful than full-thickness burns, in which the underlying tissues are damaged and nerve endings are destroyed.

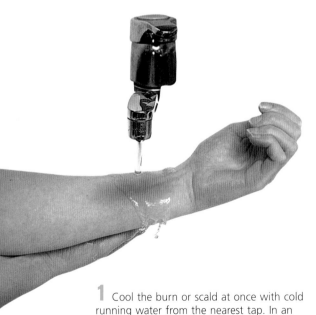

**1** Cool the burn or scald at once with cold running water from the nearest tap. In an emergency, any cold, non-flammable fluid can be used. Continue cooling with cold water for at least ten minutes, even if the burn has stopped hurting. Do not apply any lotion, ointment or oil to a burn or scald.

**2** Remove any jewellery from the burned area in case of swelling. Cover the burn with a clean, non-stick dressing to reduce the risk of infection.

**3** Do not try to remove clothing or debris stuck to the burn, since this could increase the risk of infection. Cut around any attached material and cover the burned area. If a sterile dressing is not available, use a clean plastic bag, plastic film, or any clean, non-fluffy material.

**4** While waiting for help, keep monitoring the victim's pulse and breathing and check for signs of shock. Be prepared to resuscitate if necessary. Avoid giving any food or drink, unless the burn is very small, in case an anaesthetic may be needed. Monitor the victim's breathing, especially after smoke inhalation, and be prepared to give CPR (cardiopulmonary resuscitation) if necessary.

## ⊕ FIRST AID

Do not burst any blisters that form after a burn or scald as this increases the risk of infection.

Seek medical help for all but the most minor burn. If the burn is deep or covers an area greater than the size of the victim's own palm, call an ambulance.

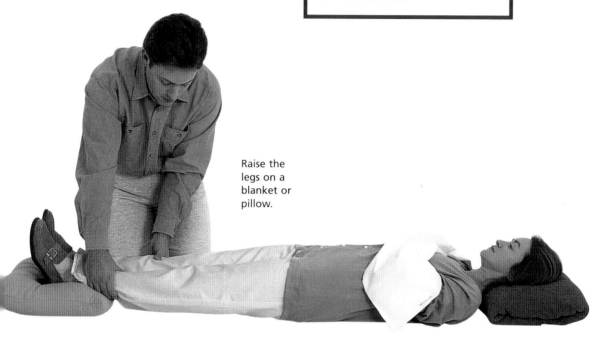

Raise the legs on a blanket or pillow.

## TREATMENT FOR BURNS AND SCALDS

**Chemical burn** First, make the area safe. Flood the burnt part with water for at least 20 minutes (this is double the time for a heat burn). Meanwhile, call an ambulance and monitor breathing – be prepared to resuscitate the victim if necessary. Remove contaminated clothing gently. Send details of the chemical involved in the accident to hospital with the victim.

**Electrical burn** Electricity, including a lightning strike, leaves burns both where the current enters and leaves the body. There is a high risk of cardiac arrest. Make sure the power source is safe before approaching the victim. Call an ambulance immediately, then treat burn injuries by cooling while waiting for help. If cardiac arrest occurs, perform CPR until the ambulance arrives.

**Burns to the airway** Burns to the face or inhalation of smoke in a fire can be very dangerous. The victim may suffer pain and extensive swelling of the lining of the mouth and throat, resulting in the narrowing or closure of the upper airway. This can be life threatening. Call an ambulance at once if you know the victim has inhaled smoke or if you notice soot or damaged skin around the mouth or nose, swelling of the mouth or tongue, or breathing difficulties. Observe the victim closely in case CPR is needed.

# Gas and smoke inhalation

Exhaust fumes and smoke from fires are every bit as deadly as the flames themselves. It is essential that you can recognise the injuries and know how to act to help the victim.

## WHAT TO LOOK FOR

- **Breathing difficulty or breathing failure**
- **Confusion, listlessness or 'drunken' behaviour**
- **Abnormal colour, including pale, blueish or cherry-pink skin**
- **Burns or soot around the mouth and nose**

Carbon monoxide from exhaust fumes or faulty heating appliances is the gas most likely to be inhaled accidentally. This can lead to serious illness, or even death. In most cases, victims of a fire will have inhaled smoke, which may include poisonous fumes given off by burning synthetic fabrics and wall coverings.

**1** Do not put yourself in danger. Unless there is a fire, ventilate an enclosed space by opening any doors and windows before entering. If the victim is conscious, help him or her out of the contaminated area into fresh air.

**2** Lift or drag an unconscious victim into the fresh air. Check the airway and begin CPR if necessary. Once breathing is regular, place the victim in the recovery position.

**3**  If the victim is conscious, monitor his or her pulse and breathing until the ambulance arrives. In the meantime, treat any other injuries, such as burns.

### ✚ FIRST AID

Send someone to call an ambulance as soon as possible. Medical assessment is vital, because serious complications can result from the inhalation of a toxic substance.

Do not enter a confined space filled with gas or smoke without proper safety equipment – await the arrival of the emergency services.

# Top ten fire hazards in the home

Being armed with information can help you to reduce the risk of fire in your home. You may well know the basics but it's worth keeping alert to hidden dangers. See if you are guilty of any of the habits listed here – and resolve to change them now. Your life could depend on it.

**1** Leaving a candle burning when there is no adult in the room.

**2** Tea towel positioned too close to the kitchen hob.

**3** Toaster being used beneath a kitchen cabinet.

**4** Cigarette left smouldering in an overflowing ashtray.

**5** Lighter or matches left lying around where children could find them.

**6** Fireplace in use without a fireguard A guard is essential for child safety.

**7** Mirror above fireplace There is a risk that the clothing of people using the mirror could be set alight by a spark or come into contact with the flames directly.

## SMOKING HAZARDS

Smoking and smoking materials are the second biggest cause of fires in the home. Every three days someone dies from a fire caused by a cigarette. If anyone in your household smokes, then they need to be aware of the fire risks and take steps to avoid them.

• Never smoke in bed – you could fall asleep whilst holding a lit cigarette.
• Don't smoke if you feel sleepy – again, you could doze off whilst holding a lit cigarette.
• Don't leave a lit cigarette or cigar unattended. It could burn down and fall on the carpet.
• Don't leave matches or lighters where children can reach them.
• Don't leave an ashtray on the arm of a chair.
• At bedtime, empty all ashtrays into a metal bin outdoors.
• Never tap ash into a wastepaper basket.
• Use a heavy ashtray that will not tip over.

**8** Pans cooking on the hob or an iron left on with no adult supervision.

**9** Frayed cords on electrical appliances.

**10** Overloaded sockets that can cause an electrical fire.

# Safety equipment

Many DIY activities generate dust, debris, fumes, noise and heat. Before starting, buy a personal protective equipment (PPE) kit. These are available from DIY outlets and include safety goggles, a dust mask, ear defenders and gloves.

**Ear defenders** or ear plugs made to British Standard BS EN 352-4:2001 will protect your hearing during noisy jobs, such as sanding a floor, using a chainsaw or drilling masonry.

**Safety goggles** or spectacles made to British Standard BS EN 166:2002 will protect you from eye injuries when drilling, sawing, sanding, driving in masonry nails or using chemicals, especially when working above head height.

**A disposable face mask** will stop you from inhaling the coarse, airborne, non-toxic dust and particles caused by many drilling, sawing and sanding jobs. If you are spraying paint or creating toxic dust, you should wear a specialist mask made to British Standard BS EN 140:1999.

## ADVICE FOR SAFE DIY

- Keep the room well ventilated when you are painting or using any material that generates toxic fumes.
- Use the correct tools for the job.
- If using a power drill, ensure it has a plastic, non-conducting body. Unplug it before swapping parts.
- When using a knife, always cut away from your body. Make sure knives are stored securely, too.
- Switch off the power before fixing or checking electrical connections, and unplug electrical appliances. Wear rubber-soled shoes when working on anything electrical.
- Erect ladders according to manufacturers' instructions, and never lean out to one side of them – ladders are one of the main causes of DIY accidents every year.
- Take your time and don't rush jobs – this is when accidents occur.
- Consult a professional if you are unsure what you are doing.

**Gloves** protect your hands when handling coarse building materials or working with chemicals that could harm your skin. Use leather gloves for building and gardening work; PVC ones when handling chemicals. Disposable latex gloves can provide useful light-weight protection for many dirty but not potentially harmful jobs.

# Harmful substances

Every household includes a store of chemicals for a vast range of purposes, from toilet cleaner to paint stripper indoors; weedkiller to engine oil outside. You need to know which are harmful, and what to do in the event of an accident.

Many commonplace household and garden chemicals are poisonous – and potentially lethal if swallowed by a child. They can also damage the environment if not disposed of safely. Before using any chemical, read the instructions. Observe any safety warnings, such as 'do not use near naked flame' or 'always use in a well-ventilated area', and never use a chemical for anything other than the purpose for which it is intended. Keep separate instruction leaflets in a file for future reference.

Use your PPE kit when dealing with harmful substances and never leave chemicals where children can reach them.

Contact your local authority waste disposal department for advice on disposing of chemicals safely.

## Paints and varnishes

Solvent-based paints can release volatile organic compounds when applied, and for several days afterwards. These can cause serious health problems, including eye, nose, throat and lung irritation. Although new legislation limits solvent levels, it is still essential to keep a room well ventilated during redecoration.

Some varnishes, too, give off strong, dangerous fumes, especially acid catalyst varnish. Always wear a mask that protects against vapour when varnishing, and keep children and pets well out of the way.

## Patio cleaners

These heavy-duty masonry cleaners contain up to ten per cent hydrochloric acid – HCl, also known as muriatic acid. This is a highly

reactive liquid acid and one of the most dangerous chemicals you can buy for home use.

Muriatic acid can damage most things it touches, including clothing, metal and skin. It gives off an unpleasant odour and this will badly burn the lining of the nose, throat and lungs.

Do not use a cleaner containing hydrochloric acid unless you have no other choice. There are alternative cleaners available, such as those containing phosphoric acid, which is a lot less dangerous, or a water-only jet wash may be sufficient.

## Loft insulation

Insulating products – especially loft insulation made from glass-fibre – can act as an irritant. Only open the packaging in the loft, and keep the hatch door closed while you are working. Wear protective gloves and overalls or a long-sleeved shirt, tucking sleeves and trouser legs into gloves and socks. If fibres do get into the gloves, they will cause more irritation than if you had worn no gloves in the first place. Wear a suitable face mask and throw it away after use.

## Avoiding asbestos

Until the 1970s, asbestos was commonly used in building materials to make them stronger and more fire retardent; it was also common in insulating materials. Once installed, these products do not pose a risk, but breaking up boards or insulation to remove them can release potentially dangerous asbestos fibres, so it is important to be aware of the dangers when embarking on DIY projects around your home. If you are in any doubt about asbestos in your home, seek advice from your local council's Environmental Health Department.

Do not attempt DIY on sprayed coatings, pipe lagging or insulating boards – these materials should be handled only by a licensed asbestos-removal contractor. If you do DIY work involving contact with asbestos fibres, wear a facemask – soak the material with water first – and avoid using power tools.

Do not use a domestic vacuum cleaner to remove dust – hire a commercial one if necessary. Bag up the damp dust and offcuts in heavy-duty refuse sacks and mark them 'ASBESTOS', then contact your local authority waste disposal department for advice on its safe removal.

Decorative coatings such as Artex (below), Pebblecoat and Wondertex used to contain chrysotile asbestos. Do not attempt to sand the wall or ceiling smooth. Modern

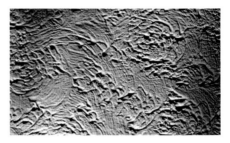

textured coatings can be removed with specialist paint removal products or a steam stripper, but if these do not work then your coating is probably the older kind. If possible, paint, cover or plaster over the Artex rather than trying to remove it; there are products on the market designed to cover textured surfaces. Alternatively, if the coating covers plasterboard, you could remove the board and replace it.

## Make your cupboards safe

The best protection you can give your household is to have a rigorous clear out of all potentially harmful substances. Check the utility room, bathroom cabinet, under the sink, the shed, greenhouse and garage. Collect together anything that is past its use-by date or has lost its label. Also, get rid of old garden chemicals – they may now have deteriorated and could even be banned for home use. Take your haul to your local waste-disposal site and hand it over to a member of staff.

# Protect children from poisons in your home

Most cases of accidental poisoning involve children, so it's important to make sure all poisonous substances are safely stored out of their reach.

**Household cleaning products** are often stored under the sink in a low cupboard, within easy reach of little hands. Fit a lock or a childproof catch to the cupboard, or move the items out of reach. Keep all cleaning fluids in their original containers – never transfer them into old drink bottles.

**Alcohol** must be kept locked away – a large swig of neat spirits could kill a toddler. Screwing the lid on very tightly may not be enough to keep out a determined child.

**Tobacco** can be lethal to a child. A single cigarette, if swallowed, could kill a one-year-old.

**Small batteries** such as the mercury disc batteries used in some watches, electronic games and hearing aids, can be easily swallowed so keep these out of children's reach. Do your best to make sure that children know never to put them in their mouths, ears or up their noses.

**Medicines** should always be kept out of children's reach. Store tablets, inhalers, syrups and other liquid medicines – particularly children's medicines, which often taste appealingly sweet – in a locked cupboard, even if the containers have child-resistant lids.

Herbal medicines and vitamin pills can also be dangerous in the wrong dosage, so keep these out of reach, too.

**Plants** can be hazardous. The leaves, berries, flowers or fruit of some common house and garden plants, such as foxgloves, are poisonous when eaten (see box below). Teach children never to eat anything from the garden unless you are with them and have told them that it is safe.

**Garden chemicals** including weedkillers, fertilisers, barbecue lighters and methylated spirits should be kept locked in the garden shed or garage. Paint thinner and paint remover, petrol, paraffin and metal polishes should also be locked away.

**Guests and visitors** may be less alert to children's tendency to put things in their mouths. Make sure visitors never leave pills, inhalers or other medicines accessible in the bathroom or in an open bag. Likewise, when you visit other people, whose home may not be as childproof as your own, keep a close eye on your children.

---

## POISONOUS PLANTS

Many house or conservatory plants can be toxic, as can garden plants, especially laurel, rue, privet and yew berries, and laburnum seeds. Be particularly careful with plants that have berries, which are attractive to children. Here are some of the more commonly found poisonous plants:

Autumn crocus (*Colchicum*)
Castor oil plant (*Ricinus communis*)
Deadly nightshade (*Atropa*)
False hellebore (*Veratrum*)
Foxglove (*Digitalis*)
Honeysuckle (*Lonicera*) (berries)
Laburnum
Leopard lily (*Dieffenbachia*)
Lily-of-the-valley (*Convallaria majalis*)
Lords and ladies (*Arum*)
Mistletoe
Monkshood (*Aconitum*)
Oleander
Philodendron
Poinsettia
Rhododendron
Rhubarb (leaves)
Tomato (leaves)
Wisteria
Woody nightshade (*Solanum dulcamara*)
Yew (*Taxus*)

**SAFETY**

# Poison that has been absorbed or inhaled

Quick identification of a poisoning incident and swift action to deal with it can save lives – especially if the victim is a child.

## WHAT TO LOOK FOR

### Poison absorbed

- An irritating rash at the contact site
- Moderate to severe pain at contact site
- Nausea, headache or dizziness
- Area of redness, blisters or a rash
- Distress

### Poison inhaled

- Breathing difficulty or breathing failure
- Listlessness, confusion or 'drunken' behaviour
- Abnormal colour, including pale, cherry-pink or blueish skin
- Distress

## Absorbed poisons

Some substances found around the home can be highly toxic if absorbed through the skin. These include insecticides and weedkillers. Household chemicals can also cause severe contact burns.

1 Ask the victim to remove all contaminated clothing immediately.

2 Wash affected areas of skin thoroughly under running water.

## Inhaled poisons

There are many substances around the home from which poisonous fumes can be inhaled accidentally. In a fire, smoke from burning plastics and synthetic furnishings is likely to contain toxic vapours. Carbon monoxide from faulty heating appliances can also cause severe poisoning.

1 If the victim is conscious, help them out of the contaminated area into fresh air.

2 Drag an unconscious victim away by the feet or shoulders. Keep the victim under close observation outside until the ambulance arrives.

 **FIRST AID**

If a victim becomes unconscious after absorbing or inhaling poison, check the airway and be ready to begin CPR (cardiopulmonary resuscitation). Place the victim in the recovery position (see page 27) once they are breathing and have regained a pulse and monitor them until help arrives. Send someone to call an ambulance as soon as possible.

# Poison that has been swallowed

Children are most likely to swallow poison, and it is vital to discover what poison has been consumed, how great a quantity and when.

## WHAT TO LOOK FOR

- Nausea
- Abdominal cramps
- Vomiting
- Seizures or convulsions
- Burns around the mouth and nose
- Diarrhoea
- Drowsiness or loss of consciousness
- Confusion or hallucinations
- A used container; berries

## Poison taken by mouth

Poison is most often taken by mouth, especially by young children. If a poison has been swallowed, do not give any food or fluid unless directed to do so, as this can cause complications.

**1** If the victim is conscious, ask what type of poison has been taken, how much and how long ago.

**2** If there is any redness or signs of burning around the mouth or on the lips, wash the area well with plenty of cold water.

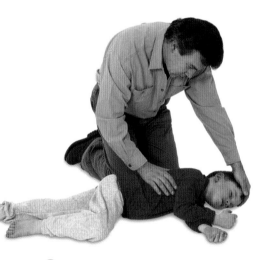

**3** If the victim is unconscious, check the airway. If necessary, begin CPR promptly. Avoid contamination by using a plastic face shield, if available. Place the victim in the recovery position (see below) until medical help arrives.

## ✚ FIRST AID

Call an ambulance AT ONCE.
Send any samples of poison or vomit to the hospital with the victim.
Do not try to induce vomiting, the victim could choke.

## Avoiding accidents

• Keep dangerous substances out of sight and out of reach of children.
• Keep all medications in a locked medicine cabinet.
• Chemicals should be left in their original, correctly labelled containers and should never be mixed or transferred into food or soft drink containers that might be attractive to a child.
• Never mix cleaning products together. Store them in a locked cupboard or on a shelf that is inaccessible to children.
• Keep all medicines and household substances in childproof containers.
• Return out-of-date medicines or those no longer needed to a pharmacy so that they can be disposed of safely.

# Working safely outdoors

Follow these precautions to keep yourself safe when you are carrying out DIY jobs outside the house or in the garden.

## Use tools safely

Many DIY tools need sharp blades or powerful motors to do their jobs properly. This means that they can cause injury if they are not used with care. Keep bladed tools sharp so they will cut without effort, and make sure that your hands are behind the cutting direction and out of the cutting line. Read the instructions before using any power tool for the first time, and never bypass or de-activate any safety guard that is fitted to the tool.

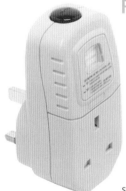

## Power tools in the garden

If you are using a power tool outdoors, you must plug it into a socket outlet or adaptor fitted with a residual current device (RCD). If the RCD detects an imbalance in the power supply because of faulty insulation or because someone has touched a live part, the RCD will switch off the supply immediately – fast enough to prevent an electric shock from being fatal.

## Carrying heavy loads

Take care when lifting heavy items such as paving slabs. Stand close to whatever you are lifting, with your feet apart and your back straight. Squat down so you can grip the load. Then straighten your legs and stand up as you lift, keeping the load as close to your body as possible. If something is too heavy or awkward to lift alone, get help or look into the range of lifting equipment that can be hired. This includes items such as panel lifters, barrows for carting flagstones around the garden, and manual grabs for handling bricks.

## Wear the right safety gear

Assemble a safety kit before embarking on DIY work. For many outdoor jobs, you will need a hard hat, a pair of strong work gloves and sturdy footwear. You should also have safety goggles, a face mask and, if you intend to use noisy power tools for long periods, some ear protectors too. For work on the roof, a tool pouch ensures you have both hands free for climbing the ladder (above) and reduces the chances of tools sliding down the roof and injuring anyone on the ground below.

## NEW WIRING REGULATIONS

Since January 2005, all new domestic wiring work in England and Wales must comply with the requirements of a new section of the Building Regulations. Part P, entitled Electrical Safety, covers design, installation, inspection and testing of electrical work in the home. It applies to both professional and DIY electrical work.

If you install any new outdoor circuit, such as one supplying garden lighting or an outbuilding, you must notify your local authority building control department before you start work. When the job is completed the local authority will inspect and test your work for a fee of around £100–£200. They will then issue you with a Building Regulations Self-certification Certificate and an Electrical Installation Certificate. If you are in any doubt as to whether the work you plan to do requires notification, contact your local authority building control department for advice.

## Safety on the rooftop

**Have a helper to hand** When you are working at a height make sure you have a helper with you. Ask them to steady the weight at the bottom of the ladder when you are carrying up heavy items.

**Have a safe place to put your tools** Fix a tray to a ladder or hold tools in a bag or pouch slung across your chest, or wear a tool belt (left).

**Lower debris to the ground** Use a stout sack or bucket attached to a rope to lower anything to the ground. Take care not to drop anything; it could cause serious injury.

## Using ladders safely

**Secure a firm foothold** If a ladder is going to be in one position for a lengthy job, tie it to sturdy pegs driven into the ground on each side of the uprights to prevent it slipping. On hard surfaces, or when you need to move the ladder frequently, get someone to stand on the bottom rung to anchor the ladder in place while you work.

On soft ground, stand the ladder on a board to stop it from sinking. Screw a batten to the board to prevent the ladder from sliding outwards, then tie and stake it. Alternatively, you can hire a ladder safety foot, with a high-friction base (below).

With the ladder set up, climb three rungs and jump up and down, then lean out to each side to check that it won't settle. Reposition the ladder on firmer ground or on a board if it moves.

**A safe footing** One of the most useful accessories for improving ladder safety is a safety foot (below), which can be bought or hired. The high-friction base resists slipping when the ladder is standing on a hard surface. It also spreads the load and stops the feet of the ladder from sinking into soft ground.

**Get a good grip** Hold the rungs, not the ladder sides, when you climb or descend a ladder. If you miss your footing, you will automatically grab them and so avoid a fall. If you hold the sides and you slip, you will get skin burns from a metal ladder and splinters from a wooden one. Don't hug the ladder; climb with your arms straight and your body upright.

**Stand well away** Fit a stand-off to the top of your ladder to hold it away from overhanging eaves and allow you to work on the gutters. You may crack a plastic gutter if you rest a ladder against it.

**Change to cordless** Power cables hanging from ladders are a potential safety hazard; use cordless power tools whenever you can.

**Don't climb too high** Use the top four rungs of a ladder as handholds only. If you try to stand on them and grab something higher up for support, such as a gutter or sill, you are quite likely to fall.

# Using power tools outdoors

Electricity in the garden can kill. Always connect any mains-powered equipment via a residual current device (RCD), which helps to protect you from the risk of electrocution.

An RCD provides protection against the risk of shock if you cut through an extension lead and touch a live wire. It detects and reacts to changes in the flow of electricity, so if a flex or cable is cut, or the tool malfunctions, the RCD cuts off the power supply to the equipment. Safety switches on power tools are there for a reason – don't try to override them. Keep tools with sharp edges out of the reach of children; better still, lock them away.

If you've got a shed, it is important to keep it tidy – this will help you to reach the tools you want without risking an accident. Get into the habit of unplugging and putting electrical equipment such as lawnmowers and hedge trimmers away as soon as you have finished using them. Do not clean, adjust or even check power tools that are plugged in. Never use mains-powered tools in the wet or wash them with water: you risk electrocution.

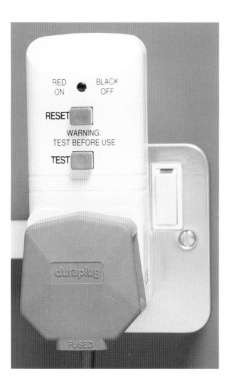

## CARE WITH CABLES

Tripping over a trailing cable is one of the main causes of accidents involving power tools – or even vacuum cleaners – in the home and garden. A new and simple cable grip, called the Grass Snake, helps to avoid this, by looping the cable up to your waist and allowing it to trail safely behind you. It also minimises the risk of accidentally cutting through cable itself with a hedge trimmer or electric lawnmower. One end of the clip hooks through a belt loop on your clothing while the other end has a ridged clip to grip cables of a variety of thicknesses.

## Using garden power tools

- Always use an RCD.
- Always disconnect power tools before touching their blades.
- Keep the cable behind you while you work, and don't allow it to become kinked.
- Never work in damp or wet conditions.
- Use brightly coloured leads – they are easy to see and avoid.
- Wear strong shoes or boots.
- When you hire equipment always make sure that the hire shop staff show you how it works – even if you think you are already familiar with the tool.
- Always wear appropriate safety clothing – a hire shop will sell PPE (personal protective equipment) kits for use with power tools (see page 54).

# Using a chainsaw safely

A chainsaw is one of the most dangerous garden tools. It can cause horrific injuries, especially if you have no experience of using one.

Any adult is permitted to use a chainsaw in his or her own garden, but this is not wise unless you have been carefully shown how to use one properly by an expert. The manufacturer's instructions are not enough.

Maintenance checks must be made every time you use a chainsaw. If these are not carried out, the tool could prove hard to control and even cause serious injury. The vibration generated when the chainsaw is in use can, for example, loosen screws and nuts securing safety features such as front and rear hand guards, and also affect the tension of the chain.

## Protect yourself

Staff at the tool hire or garden centre will be able to advise you as to what protective gear you should wear. Generally, a safety helmet, goggles, steel toecap boots and clothing made from protective material should be worn.

Never use a chainsaw if you have been drinking alcohol or you feel tired – you need quick reactions.

Always keep people away from where you're working and store the chainsaw safely after use.

## Safety guidelines for using a chainsaw

• Apply the saw to the top of the log you are cutting, not from underneath.
• Cut using the part of the saw nearest to the motor end – it's easier to control.
• Do not carry the saw about with its motor running, even if the blade is disengaged.
• Keep the chain at the correct tension, or it could fly off.
• Sharpen frequently – a blunt saw causes the user to exert too much pressure.
• Only fill a petrol-powered saw when the engine is cold, or the petrol could ignite.
• Wear appropriate protective clothing, gauntlets and sturdy shoes.
• Make sure your work area is clear so that

## BEWARE OF KICKBACK

Kickback is a sudden uncontrolled upward movement of the chainsaw's guide bar. It happens when the nose of the guide bar hits an object. It causes many chainsaw injuries, especially to the face and upper body, which are difficult to protect. To minimise the likelihood of kickback:

• Don't allow the guide bar nose to touch any obstruction
• Don't over-reach
• Keep the saw below chest height
• Keep the thumb of your left hand around the back of the front handle
• Always saw at full power.

nothing can catch on the blade or trigger.
• Keep people at least 10m away when you are working.
• Unplug the mains lead or disconnect the spark plug lead before cleaning or adjusting the saw.
• Have the saw serviced regularly. If you hire a chainsaw, look for a tag on the tool, stating that it has been serviced and tested since it was last returned to the shop.

OUTDOORS

# Child safety in the garden

Take a look at your garden and see which parts are, or could be, safe play areas. Then look again, from a child's point of view, and see if you can spot potential danger zones. Some hazards are obvious, others less so.

**Garden soil** If you or your neighbours have pets that mess in the garden, keep a look out and clear it up whenever you spot it. But the soil may also contain wild animal faeces, so it's a good idea to make sure your child always washes his or her hands after playing outside.

**Leaves, flowers, berries or bulbs** Some parts of some plants are poisonous and should not be eaten; other plants can irritate the skin if touched. For this reason young children should be taught not to pick or put any parts of plants into their mouths.

**Washing lines** A less obvious hazard is the garden washing line. Rotary washing lines can be a hazard when closed, as a child playing with the line could get tangled in it – and even be strangled. If you have this type of washing line, keep it erect or lock it in the garden shed when not in use.

**Boundaries** Check that your garden boundary is secure so that children cannot escape. This means that gates must be lockable and too high to climb over, and fences secure, with no gaps that a toddler might squeeze through. Your garden may be safe, but next door could have a pond, a water butt, an unlocked shed or a gate open to the road.

**Barbecues** A barbecue or chimnaea gets hot very quickly and will burn a child's hands if touched. Even after the fire has gone out, the charcoal can stay hot for hours.
Never leave children alone with a barbecue, and make sure that even the youngest understand that it is very hot, and will stay hot even after everyone has finished cooking and eating. Keep lighter fuels and matches out of reach.

## Water in the garden

Drowning is the third largest cause of accidental death in the home for under fives. Most cases happen in summer when the paddling pools come out, but permanent ornamental ponds and even water butts are also a hazard that must be well protected.
A child can drown in moments in less than 3cm of water. Never leave your child unattended near any kind of water. In summer, empty the pool at the end of playtime each day.
If you have a pond and small children, consider filling it in until they are older or fence it off securely. A rigid cover of strong chicken wire stretched over a sturdy wooden frame and secured over the water is also a solution to prevent children falling in. Positioning groups of pots or deep flowerbeds around the pond will help to avoid children running into the pond without noticing it, but a more likely cause of accidents is a child toppling in as they lean over to look for fish, frogs and other pond creatures. Be especially vigilant in other people's gardens.

### DON'T TURN YOUR BACK

If you have toddlers you'll know how quickly they can move. Never believe that you can nip off to answer the phone or make a pot of tea and leave a mobile toddler in the garden. Take him with you. A newly walking child does not have the physical competence to save himself from danger. This advice is especially crucial when visiting friends – their garden may not be as child friendly as yours. Remember, 80 per cent of pond drownings happen in other people's gardens.

## Garden tools and equipment

All garden tools, from secateurs to strimmers, are fascinating to children. Many are sharp, heavy or both, and should be kept locked away when not in use. Other tempting and potentially dangerous garden paraphernalia – twine, bamboo canes and wire, for example – should also be stored in a locked shed, as should weedkiller, fertiliser, slug pellets and other garden chemicals.

## Garden toys

Make sure that all the toys your children play with in the garden conform to the current safety standards and are suitable for your child's age. A sandpit should have a lid (above) to stop pets or wildlife using it as a litter tray, and should be sited in a lightly shaded area, such as under a tree.

Swings, climbing frames and other play equipment should be sensibly positioned and secure. It's important to check large equipment regularly to make sure that no bolts or fittings have worked loose.

You can minimise the risk of bumps and bruises by creating a soft surface beneath a swing, trampoline or climbing frame. The simplest surface is a layer of bark chips (below) at least 50mm thick. Lay a weed suppressing membrane first, then all the surface needs is raking occasionally and topping up with fresh bark.

## TRAMPOLINES

Trampolines are a relatively recent craze, and for parents relieved to get their children away from the games console and exercising out of doors, a terrific one. However, the boom in trampolining has led to an increase in accidents. Follow these simple guidelines for happy, healthy and safe trampolining.

Buy a model with safety pads that completely cover the springs, hooks and frame. Consider ones with safety netting as part of the design, or buy a safety cage to reduce the chance of your child falling off the trampoline and hitting the ground.

Place the trampoline on a soft surface such as a springy lawn or a thick bed of bark chippings (see below left), never on a hard surface.

Ban access via a ladder, which could be used by small children.

Write out the list of rules below, laminate it and stick it up somewhere visible near the trampoline:
• Take turns – only one at a time, ALWAYS.
• No somersaults or flips.
• Bounce in the middle.
• Never jump off. Stop bouncing and climb down.
• Keep back when someone else is jumping.
• Never go underneath the trampoline if someone is jumping.
• If you see a split in the mat or the padding has moved off the springs, don't use the trampoline – tell an adult.

# Outdoor sockets

Water and electricity are a dangerous combination, so special switches and sockets with hinged weatherproof covers are essential for providing power to lawnmowers, pond pumps and garden lighting.

The outdoor socket or switch is wired in the same way as a conventional indoor socket or switch, but must be connected to the ring main via a residual current device (RCD) on a spur running from an indoor socket outlet circuit. If the new outlet has an integral RCD, it can be connected directly to the ring main at a socket outlet or junction box.

Run PVC cable to the desired location indoors, then route it through a hole drilled in the wall and wire straight into the back of the new box. Use conduit to protect the cable where it is exposed outdoors (below).

Drain holes in the base of the mounting box allow condensation build-up to escape, while a spring-hinged weatherproof cover prevents rainwater from entering the terminals of the socket outlet.

When a power supply is being run to an outbuilding, it must not be fed from a spur, but must have a dedicated circuit wired from the consumer unit. Before having any wiring installed outdoors, read the information on Wiring Regulations on pages 16–17.

## SAFETY WARNING

To avoid digging through cables, outdoor cabling to a shed or outhouse should be buried at least 600mm underground. Armoured cable needs no further protection, but PVC cable must be run through conduit.

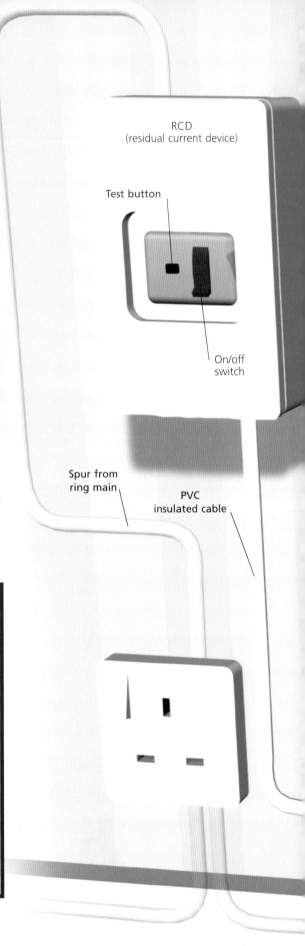

RCD (residual current device)

Test button

On/off switch

Spur from ring main

PVC insulated cable

## MAINTENANCE AND FAULTS

### Before each use

Press the test button on the RCD to check that it is operating correctly before you use it. Then press reset or move the switch back to the 'on' position to restore the power.

### If the tool does not work

The most likely cause of failure of a tool to work is that the power to the socket is off. Check that the RCD has not tripped and that it has been correctly reset after your pre-use check (above). Then check the MCB or fuse serving the circuit in the main consumer unit. Reset a tripped MCB or replace a blown fuse if necessary. If the RCD trips repeatedly, there is probably a fault with the tool. Stop using it immediately and get it repaired.

## CLEANING THE SOCKET

Once a year, clean the mounting box and cover. Turn off the outdoor extension by switching the RCD to 'off'. Using a clean, damp cloth, wipe the exterior surfaces of the socket and cover. Restore the power. Apply a small amount of grease to each of the spring hinges (above). This will keep the action free and displace water to prevent rusting.

**Weatherproof cover**

**Outdoor socket outlet**

**Mounting box**

**Conduit (covering cable)**

# Safety in the kitchen

**Sharp knives, hot water, electrical appliances, a hob and household chemicals all in one room – it's hardly surprising that so many accidents happen in kitchens.**

Kitchen accidents range from cuts and bruises to burns and poisoning. A well-designed, tidy kitchen is a big step towards eliminating risk. These sensible practices will also help make your kitchen safe.

**Knives** Keep knives sharp – a blunt knife is dangerous as it requires more pressure and is therefore more likely to slip and cut you.

Never use a knife to cut something you are holding in your hand – always use a sturdy chopping board. If you put a damp cloth under the board it will give it a good grip – if the board were to slide suddenly you could easily cut yourself.

Store knives in a knife block or on a magnetic wall rack, not jumbled with other

cutlery in a drawer. Other sharp implements should be stored in a lockable drawer. If you knock a knife off the worktop, don't try to catch it as it falls. It could slice into your hand. Instead, move out of the way and let it fall.

Wash knives separately from other utensils – never in a bowl of soapy water along with the rest of the washing up. If you put knives in the dishwasher, load them points downwards.

**Kitchen storage** When storing items in cupboards, don't put heavy items on high shelves. Use proper kitchen steps or a rubber-topped hop-up to access items on high shelves. Keep food cupboards clean, tidy and dry. Make a habit of shutting cupboard doors and drawers every time you use them.

**Gas safety** If your central heating boiler is in the kitchen, make sure there is adequate ventilation and that vents and flues are not blocked. Fit a carbon monoxide detector – this dangerous gas has no smell and can kill. As for smoke detectors, test them regularly and change the battery as advised. Have the boiler serviced every year by a CORGI-registered engineer.

**Electrical safety** Never turn on switches or plug in appliances with wet hands. Don't overload sockets – ideally, restrict yourself to no more than one plug to each socket – and check plugs and flexes regularly.

Be aware that since new Building Regulations were introduced in 2005, domestic electric jobs in kitchens must be carried out by a registered electrician or be approved and certified by your local authority Building Control department (see pages 16–17).

**Child safety** As soon as a baby begins to move around and walk, you need to buy a playpen – and use it – or get down to his level and see what he could reach and pull down. The flexes from kettles and other appliances are especially tempting: keep them well away from the edge of the worktop.

When cooking, use the back burners of the stove top wherever possible and always turn the handles of pans on the front rings towards the back of the cooker.

Teach children that the cooker is dangerous and do not let them play near it, even when it is not in use. Always put hot pans, bowls and cooking utensils at the back of the worktop or in the middle of a table – not near the edge. The same applies to hot drinks.

grow. Use a separate bucket and cloth for cleaning floors – and always clean up grease or oil spills immediately so that no-one falls on the slippery floor.
• Keep raw and cooked foods apart in the fridge with raw placed at the bottom to aviod the risk of juices from uncooked meats dripping onto other food.
• To avoid cross-contamination in the fridge, cover all foods in cling film or store them in sealed boxes or tubs.
• Shop for food as regularly as possible, buying little and often, and always go home and unpack and refrigerate fresh goods straight away.
• Food poisoning can occur when hot food is left for too long at room temperature to cool off. Cool it as quickly as possible and put it in the refrigerator.
• Keep pets and their feeding bowls away from kitchen surfaces.

Store all household cleaning products out of reach or in a lockable cupboard, and never decant household chemicals into old drinks bottles. If you keep medicines or nutritional supplements in the kitchen, put them on the top shelf of a wall-mounted cupboard or in a lockable cupboard.

It is a good idea to fit child-proof catches to all kitchen base units (above). This not only keeps children safe from dangerous chemicals, it also prevents them from playing with heavy or breakable items, such as plates or dishes that could cause them an injury.

**Hygiene** Always wash your hands before and after handling food, and adopt a 'clean as you go' approach to the kitchen. After handling raw meat, poultry or fish, wash your hands, utensils and surfaces carefully and before contact with any other food – particularly cooked and ready-to-eat foods.

Use the right cleaner for the job: clean surfaces first with detergent, such as washing-up liquid, to remove any grease or dirt. Then apply disinfectant such as bleach or an anti-bacterial spray to kill any remaining germs.

Use separate cloths or sponges for separate jobs; afterwards, wash them in hot water and detergent, swish in disinfectant, rinse and allow them to dry. Do not soak dishcloths overnight – disinfectant solutions weaken and may even allow bacteria to

## MINIMISE FIRE RISK IN THE KITCHEN

Around half of all accidental fires in the home start in the kitchen. Don't become another statistic – follow these rules to stay safe.

• Never drape tea towels over the cooker.
• Never leave a lighted hob unattended.
• Turn the cooker off when you have finished using it.
• Don't let electric cables, such as the kettle lead, trail across the hob.
• Keep the grill pan clean: a build-up of fat and grease can catch fire.
• Never allow children in the kitchen unsupervised.
• Don't put anything metallic in the microwave.
• Don't overload sockets.
• Keep electric appliances and leads away from water.
• Empty crumbs out of the toaster regularly and don't stand it near curtains or the kitchen-roll dispenser.
• Keep a fire blanket handy for fat or oil fires.
• Replace the chip pan with a thermostatically controlled electric deep-fat fryer.

# Safety in the bathroom

The bathroom, along with the kitchen, is one of the most potentially hazardous areas of the home. Take these commonsense measures to make your bathroom safer.

As electricity and water don't mix, the bathroom poses many possible dangers. Ensure that all the special requirements for electrical installations in bathrooms are met. Scalding water, unprotected razors, loose mats, wet tiles and a slippery bath are other potential dangers you should address.

Grab rails This type of support makes a big difference to safety for an elderly or infirm person. Rails can be fitted near the bath, the shower and beside the toilet and can also double as towel rails (below). Make sure that rails are securely fitted and that the wall is strong enough to take the weight – a partition wall may not be sturdy enough, even if the correct fixings are used to attach the rail. If you are buying a new bath, choose one with rails built into the sides.

Taps Scalding is a significant risk in the bathroom. Mixer taps and shower mixers with an anti-scald safety cut-out are a good idea. These taps have the facility to set the standard maximum temperature, indicated by a button (above) to prevent accidental scalding; to turn the tap beyond this point you must depress the button as you turn.

Bath and shower When you run a bath, always run the cold water first. Never run the hot water on its own as you could scald your hand simply by testing the water temperature. Use non-slip mats in the bath and shower. A young child's bath should not be hotter than 37°C. Install a thermostatic mixing valve (shown above), which controls the temperature of the hot water coming out of a tap, or a combi-boiler with temperature controls. These will ensure that the water never gets too hot. Alternatively, use a bath thermometer or a special temperature gauge that will warn you if the water is too hot (below).

**Heaters** The surface of a radiator or other bathroom heater should not become hot enough to burn someone who falls or leans against it. Any electric heaters and water heaters must be fixed and permanently wired and controlled by a pull-cord or by a switch located outside the bathroom.

**Toilet seat** If you have very young children, it may be worth fitting a toilet lock. As unlikely as it seems, a child could drown in the water in the bowl. Raising the seat height will help the elderly or infirm; you can do this by placing a plinth beneath the seat, or you can buy a raised seat – some also come with integral arms. There are even battery or air-powered seats available to provide a little extra lift.

**Toiletries** Many familiar bathroom items can be harmful to a small child if taken in large quantities. Mouthwashes, for example, can poison a child and a lot of make-up products are toxic when eaten, so make sure these are kept out of reach. Even items as seemingly innocuous as liquid soaps should be stored out of children's reach. Packaging often makes items look good enough to drink, such as strawberry conditioner or coconut shampoo.

**Medicines** Have a lockable medicine cabinet and keep medicines in their original containers, out of reach of children.

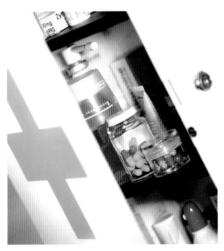

**Cleaning materials** Store toilet cleaners and bleach safely out of children's reach, and be aware of which chemicals can damage your skin. Always read and follow the instructions and advice given on cleaning products. If you think a member of your family may have swallowed or come into contact with a toxic chemical, seek medical advice. You will need to give a full description of the product and describe any symbols or guidance from the manufacturer on the bottle or package.

**Locks** A bolt or lock on a bathroom door should be too high for a child to reach. If the bathroom or toilet door locks with a key, hang this on a hook out of reach when you are not using it.

**Electricity** As far as electricity is concerned, the bathroom is the most dangerous room in the house. Water is a very efficient conductor of electrical current, and injuries caused by an electric shock will be far more severe if the victim's skin is wet. For this reason there are strict regulations governing electrical installations in bathrooms; for example, no socket outlets, other than specially designed points such as those for shavers (below), are allowed in bathrooms.

Light fittings must be appropriate to the zone in which they are located, and electrical suppliers will be able to advise you on which to choose. They must be operated with a pull-cord or a switch located outside the room.

Never use an extension lead to bring electrical items such as a hairdryer or a radio into the bathroom. Apart from the danger of plugs and leads, water vapour could condense inside the appliance's casing and make it live, exposing you to the risk of severe shock.

**Floors** Any irregular features on the floor can be a hazard, including bathmats. Make sure that bathmats are obvious by choosing a contrasting colour to the rest of the floor. If the existing bathroom floor surface is slippery – ceramic tiles, for example – consider installing a waterproof, non-slip floor covering instead, especially if young children or elderly people use the room.

# Safety in living rooms

You may have separate reception rooms, an open-plan area or perhaps a conservatory opening off the kitchen or sitting room. Whatever your living room arrangements, here are some safety guidelines.

While not posing the same risks as the kitchen or bathroom, it is essential to assess safety issues in living areas, too. According to the Royal Society for the Prevention of Accidents (ROSPA), 30,000 children trap and seriously crush their fingers in doors each year: 1,500 require surgery. Other things to watch out for are the fire, heavy furniture that could topple and glass doors.

## Using the living room safely

• Never carry hot drinks while you're holding a baby, and always put hot drinks, bowls of soup or jugs of gravy out of reach in the middle of a table, not near the edge.
• If you have tall or heavy items of furniture such as bookcases or display units, secure the tops to the wall with L-shaped brackets so they cannot topple over if they are unevenly loaded or if a child tries to climb up the shelves. Proprietary furniture straps are also available for fixing tall items back to the wall. It is a good idea to secure any item of furniture more than 1m tall.
• Do not leave candles alight in an unoccupied room or within reach of young children. Never stand candles near curtains or other flammable materials, or on the floor, and be careful not to leave matches or lighters lying around.
• Never leave a lit cigarette lying in an ashtray.
• Replace any worn carpets or rugs. You could easily trip on them. If you have wooden floors, make sure that any rugs are non slip, or backed with non-slip tape or a non-slip under rug.
• Don't tackle the ironing when a toddler is in the room – she or he could easily reach the hot iron and burn her hand or pull it on top of herself with the flex when your back is turned. Always put the iron safely out of reach after use – even a cold iron is dangerous as it is heavy.

**Fires and radiators** If you have an open fire, make sure you always use a fine mesh fireguard and get the chimney swept every year. If you have young children, use a child safety guard as well. If radiators become very hot, consider fitting radiator guards or covers – especially if you have young children or an elderly relative in the house.

**Gas appliances** If you have a gas fire, check that the flames burn blue, not yellow or orange. A gas fire that isn't burning properly can produce lethal carbon monoxide gas – which has no smell. Fit an audible carbon monoxide detector and get the fire serviced every year.

**Electrical equipment** Fit socket covers over unused electrical sockets (above right), so little fingers aren't tempted to push things into them. Never overload electric sockets with adapters and too many plugs (see page 53). Check electrical leads, plugs and sockets regularly for signs of wear and tear.

## PROTECT SMALL CHILDREN FROM ELECTRIC SHOCK

Inquisitive children are at risk through biting on electrical flexes or poking things into sockets.

- Fit guards over all unused sockets (below).
- Place lamp and appliance leads out of children's reach – perhaps behind heavy pieces of furniture.
- If a computer or stereo has a connector at the rear, make sure that a child cannot access the push-in plug and pull it out and chew it.
- Check appliances and leads for damage regularly.
- If in doubt, call a qualified electrician.

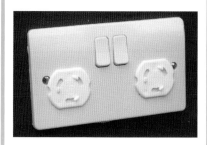

## Doors

Trapped finger accidents are common – and not just among children. The more serious accidents happen when fingers are trapped in the hinge side of doors, where they can get completely squashed as the door closes. These kinds of accidents can be prevented by fitting a hinge protection strip – a long strip of plastic that covers the narrow gap where the door joins the frame. This bends with the door as it opens, and stops children from slotting their fingers in.

Another simple way to prevent doors slamming onto fingers is to fit door jammers – spongy U-shaped devices that simply slot over the door itself (at the top or along the long edge) and stop it from shutting completely into its frame. Position them out of reach of the children they are there to protect. Be aware that old wooden doors may flex if pulled hard, so a door jammer fitted right at the top may not stop the latch from closing. Alternatively, use door wedges, but when a door is wedged open make sure it is wedged on both sides. Wedges only work with very small children, who aren't strong enough to move them.

If you want to stop a child from opening a door with a round handle, you can fit a door knob cover. This over-sized grip, which slips over the existing door knob, spins loosely round the door handle when a child tries to turn it, whereas an adult simply grips it tightly to open the door. Otherwise, simply fit a small bolt well out of reach.

## Glass

An accident can happen when someone walks or runs into a glass patio door they didn't realise was there, or falls through a glass door or window. Ordinary glass is very dangerous, as it breaks into jagged pieces.

By law, safety glass must be used in all new buildings and in glazed doors and replacement windows where the glass is less than 800mm above the floor. If you live in an older house or flat, consider replacing any glass doors or glazed panels within doors or low windows with safety glass.

A temporary – and less costly – option is to apply sticky-backed safety film to glass doors, which helps to prevent breaking glass from splintering into long and dangerous shards.

## PREVENT GLASS ACCIDENTS

A child can be frightened by breaking glass – especially if he thinks it's his fault. If an accident does happen, keep calm and try to keep the child calm, too. Clear up broken glass immediately and dispose of it safely. Here are some tricks to prevent accidents from happening:

- Apply transfers or stickers to large areas of glass, such as sliding plate-glass patio doors, to alert everyone to their presence.
- Keep loose rugs or mats away from glass doors and windows to avoid trips and falls.
- Stand plants or furniture in front of low-level glass areas.
- Keep glassed-in areas properly lit.
- When buying cabinets with glass doors or a table with a glass top, look for BS 7376 and BS 7449.

# Safety in bedrooms

About one household accident in 20 happens in a bedroom. Some involve poisoning or burns, whereas children can sustain injuries slipping or falling from bunk beds.

It may seem obvious, but don't ever smoke in bed. If you use an electric blanket, check it regularly and replace it if it is more than ten years old. Old or damaged electric blankets are a major fire risk and could also electrocute you. If the fabric is worn or the flex is damaged or frayed, replace the blanket. Always turn off an electric blanket before you get into bed.

If you have children, don't leave medicines on your bedside table – they could be mistaken for sweets. Also, leads dangling from telephones, lamps and hairdryers are a strangulation hazard and should be kept out of reach of babies and young children.

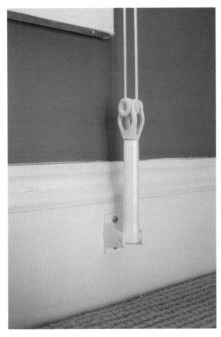

Cords used to operate blinds or curtains should be lifted high out of reach. Even cords that are held taut with tensioning devices (above) can be hazardous if they are played with. Where possible, cut the cord loop, so that the pull mechanism still works but the potential 'noose' has been eliminated.

Keep a small torch on the bedside table – moving about in the dark can be dangerous.

Keep pets out of the bedrooms. A cat trying to keep warm might climb into a baby's cot and sit on him or her; also, animals may carry fleas, threadworms and other parasites into the bedroom.

### At bedtime
Close all doors at night to stop any fires from spreading. Switch off and unplug all appliances that are not designed to stay on, including electric blankets (below).

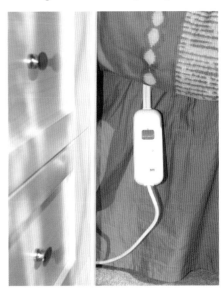

Make sure that no cigarettes or pipes are still burning and before emptying ashtrays make sure the contents are cold. Switch off any portable heaters.

## Safety in children's bedrooms

Toys Don't keep too many toys in a cot, and keep older children's toys away from the under threes – small parts can be inhaled and cause choking or be poked into ears or up noses. Be alert to small parts that could work loose or be bitten off.

Fillings in soft toys can choke young children – check that all seams are intact. Loose hair is also a choking hazard – it's safest not to give young children toys or dolls with long hair.

Tie cot toys on firmly and remove them as soon as your baby can sit up or get onto his hands and knees. Be aware that toy chests with hinged lids may trap children's fingers or fall onto their heads. Try to buy one with a safety, sliding hinge – if not, it may be possible to fit one yourself.

## BUNK BEDS

Top bunks should not be used by children under six years old. This is because the safety standards for bunk beds are based on the average measurements of a child of this age. For example, the spaces between the bars and around the mattress have been tested to make sure that a six-year-old cannot get trapped in any part of the bed.

• Think about what furniture your child could fall onto from a top bunk – and try not to put anything with sharp corners underneath.
• Put a nightlight in the bedroom, so a child needing to climb up and down in the night can do so safely.
• Discourage children from playing on the top bunk – though this may well prove futile, as most children regard bunk beds as indoor climbing frames or pirate ships.

**Temperature regulation** Use a room thermometer to help you decide how much clothing and bedding a baby needs. The ideal temperature in a baby's room is 18°C, but between 16° and 20°C is fine. Young babies cannot regulate their temperature properly; it is more dangerous for a baby to overheat than to get a bit cold. Typical signs of overheating include restlessness, sweating, damp hair, rapid breathing, heat rash and raised body temperature – the child's tummy feels hot to your touch.

Never use a hot water bottle for a baby or child – the stopper could open accidentally. You should also keep cots and beds away from radiators, heaters or direct sunlight. Avoid using quilts, baby nests, sheepskins, wedges, bedding rolls, cot bumpers and pillows – these may all cause overheating.

Move your baby into a toddler or single bed when he or she reaches two years of age or a height of 90cm (35in) – whichever comes sooner – or if he starts to climb over the sides of his cot.

**Bedguards** RoSPA (the Royal Society for the Prevention of Accidents) does not recommend the use of bedguards, as these have been known to cause injury. Instead, keep the area around the bed clear from obstructions to minimise the risk of a child being hurt should she fall out. If you are worried about bruises, put a spare mattress on the floor next to the bed for a soft landing. If you do decide to buy a bedguard, make sure it conforms to the latest safety standard – BS 7972 2001.

**Windows** Fit safety catches (below) to upstairs windows to stop them being opened far enough for a child to fall out. Different types are available for sash and casement windows. Never leave chairs or other furniture near windows where children can climb onto them.

# Safety in the hall, stairs and landing

Poor lighting, loose floor coverings, wide gaps between railings and simple clutter can all contribute to accidents in the areas that link one part of your home to another.

The largest proportion of accidents in the home involve falls from stairs or steps, and these falls are a major cause of serious injury in older people. If there are children in your home, again the stairs are an obvious hazard. Halls and landings are the ideal place for smoke alarms, as they are often in the centre of the house.

## Safety on the stairs and landings

Hand rails or banisters must be securely fitted and balusters (the upright posts) fixed in place. Measure the gaps between balusters – if they are wider than 100mm (4in), a child could squeeze through or get trapped. Large gaps should be boarded up or covered with safety netting.

Keep your stairs free from clutter and make sure stair and landing carpets are fastened down securely and have no worn or frayed patches.

If you have young children, fit stair gates both at the top and the bottom of the stairs. If another flight of stairs leads to an attic or basement, you will need to gate this, too. Make sure that you choose the right type of gate for each end of the staircase, as gates that are designed for the bottom of the stairs can be a trip hazard if fitted at the top.

Once you have fitted gates, always use them. It may be awkward shutting the gate behind you when you are carrying an armful of laundry, but the one time you don't shut the gate may be the chance your toddler grabs to climb through.

## SAFETY GATE DOS AND DON'TS

• Do fit baby gates sooner than you think you need to, so as not to get caught out by a suddenly mobile baby.
• Do buy a safety gate approved to British or European standards.
• Do follow manufacturer's instructions for secure installation.
• Do make a habit of keeping the gate shut.
• Don't buy a second-hand gate. Its catch may be worn, and it may not comply with current safety standards.
• Don't use a pressure-mounted gate at the top of the stairs.
• Don't climb over the gate if your child is watching you.
• Don't assume a gate will keep your child safe and leave him unattended.

## PREVENTING FALLS

You can fall over anything – but often it's the little things, so easily overlooked, that cause the accidents. Keep your eyes peeled for small toys, handbags, shoes and curling rug edges. Other common trip hazards are chair legs and family pets getting underfoot. The most obvious place for a fall is the stairs. We are all guilty of popping things on a step ready to take up later. Either get into the habit of putting things away and never leaving them on the stairs, or buy a special step basket that perches on a bottom step, ready to store items to be taken upstairs later.

Don't leave your keys on a hall table, either. While children hurt themselves or put them in their mouths, burglars have been known to 'fish' through the letterbox to steal house or car keys.

**Gas safety** If the gas boiler is in the hall or under the stairs, make sure it has adequate ventilation and have it serviced every year. Poisonous carbon monoxide fumes can rise and affect people sleeping upstairs. For peace of mind, fit a carbon monoxide detector within range of the boiler.

**Understairs cupboards** Often concealing electricity meters and the vacuum cleaner, the understairs cupboard is also a popular children's hiding place. But because the door catch generally opens from the outside only, a child can easily become trapped inside and panic. Sadly, this is also somewhere children tend to hide in the event of a fire. Fit a lock to the cupboard and use it, and teach children that this is not a safe place to hide or play.

**Balconies** If you like having the door to a balcony open, fix a stair gate across the opening so a small child can't get out there. Never let any child onto a balcony without supervision, and before you do, measure the gaps between the railings. If they are any wider than 100mm (4in) apart, fix safety mesh over them.

Are there any objects on the balcony that a child could stand on? Garden furniture or flowerpots could be used as a step-up, so keep these well away from the railings. It is a good idea to keep an escape ladder readily available in case of an emergency, but not accessible to children.

## Halls

If the front door or the porch area is glazed, make sure that the glass is safety glass. In an older house, this is unlikely, so have the glass replaced or cover it with safety film to stop it splintering if it breaks.

Is there a cat flap? Unless it is a recent model, replace it. Children have been known to trap their heads in older style cat flaps, while intruders may be able to access the inside lock of a door via an old-fashioned cat flap.

Keep the hall free of trip hazards, including prams, bikes, sports kit and school satchels.

Make sure that halls, stairs and landings are adequately lit. Consider leaving a low energy lamp on at night to light the way to the bathroom. If there are sockets on the landing and stairs, then buy a couple of plug-in nightlights.

# Security

# Ten ways to keep your property secure

Most break-ins are carried out by casual thieves looking for easy pickings. A thief is unlikely to persist if he encounters locked doors and windows. The tips given here will all help to keep your home secure.

**1** Deliveries Cancel milk and newspaper deliveries when you go away. Arrange for a neighbour to push post and free papers through the door and if you have a glazed porch or door, to move the post each morning so that it is not visible.

**2** Garage Add extra security to a back door inside a garage where an intruder could work totally hidden. Ensure that the garage itself is fitted with secure locks. An electronically operated, metal up-and-over door will provide the most security.

**3** Ladders Keep ladders locked away. If they must be stored outside, padlock them to a wall with special brackets.

**4** Sheds If you keep valuable equipment or tools in a shed, make sure it is securely padlocked. Tools stored there could be used for a break-in. A garden spade, for example, makes a powerful lever for opening windows. Fit a high-security padlock and secure the hasp with nuts and bolts passing through the door and frame. Replace glass with hard-to-break polycarbonate sheet, and fit window locks to opening windows – or simply screw them shut from inside.

**5** Security lights Outside lights that switch on automatically when a sensor picks up movement outside the house can be a real deterrent to crime. Site them where a burglar may try to gain access, for example high above French windows at the back or over a garage door, and fit the sensor well out of reach. A light fitted above a front door will also help you to see who is calling at night. Bear in mind that most domestic situations do not require high power floodlights, which can be a real nuisance to neighbours.

**6** Marking valuables Print your house number and post code on valuable possessions with an ultra-violet marking pen. This will help police to prove they were stolen, and assist in returning them. Metal items can be marked with hammer-and-letter punches. Photograph valuable items together, showing on the photograph where they are marked.

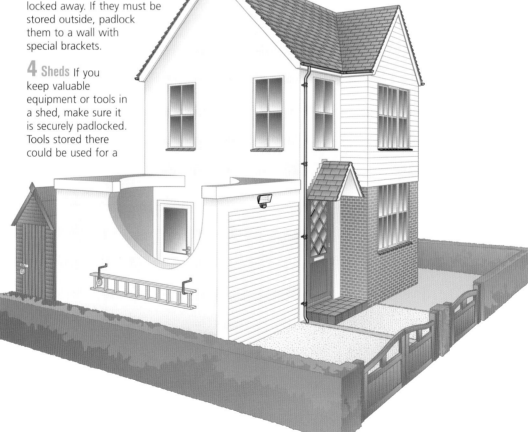

**7 Accessible windows** Never leave windows open when you go out. Security shutters will increase the safety of your property, obscuring the view inside and preventing access even if the window is broken. Fit suitable locks (see pages 92–93) to all windows, especially those with easy access – near flat roofs, drainpipes and trees. Make sure the frames are thick enough to accommodate the device; if you have plastic windows, consult the installer of your windows to find out which devices you can use.

Fitting laminated glass in windows can greatly add to the security. It consists of a sandwich of glass with a clear plastic film between. Although the glass may be cracked by a blow, the plastic will resist efforts to break through. Wired glass has little security value.

**8 Driveways** A gravel drive or path at the front of the house is a noisy surface that will alert you to the approach of visitors or intruders. For large areas, buy gravel in one tonne bulk bags which can be emptied

**GETTING POLICE HELP**

The Crime Prevention Officer at your local police station will visit you at home, point out weak spots in your security and suggest the most appropriate security measures.

If you see anyone loitering in your street or acting suspiciously, do not approach them. Call the police, then continue to watch unseen until they arrive. Neighbourhood Watch groups encourage neighbours to be alert for anything suspicious in their area. They also stress the importance of protecting property, and marking valuables. If you are interested in getting involved in a group, contact your local Crime Prevention Officer.

**THINK LIKE A THIEF**

Put yourself into the mind of a burglar. How would you break into your home if you were locked out? This is the route an intruder is most likely to take.

A burglar will look through windows to see if you have anything easily portable that's worth taking so keep valuables and keys for window locks or doors out of sight.

Close curtains and leave some timed lights on if you are going to be out after dark. During the day, consider having a radio on a timer. Noise is an even more convincing sign of occupancy than light. It may seem obvious, but always check that all windows and doors are closed and locked properly. In about a third of all break-ins, the thief gets in through an open window or door. Even if you're working in the back garden, make sure that the front door and windows are shut and locked. And if you can't see the back door from where you are working, then lock that, too.

If you come home and something looks suspicious – an open gate, an open or broken window or an open door – don't go inside. Call the police from a neighbour's house or from your mobile phone.

straight onto the drive area on delivery. One tonne of gravel will cover about 16m$^2$ (19sq yd) at a depth of 25mm.

**9 Gates** A gate at the garden boundary, particularly a locked one, is a very effective deterrent to burglars. To prevent a thief from lifting your gate off its hinges, drill a hole through one hinge pin and fit a small nut and bolt through it once the gate is hung.

**10 Keys** Never have a name-and-address tag on your keys. At most, use your surname, with a company address or the address of a relative for them to be returned to if you lose them. Be wary of leaving home to collect keys from someone who says they have found them. It may be a ruse to get you out of the house while the keys are used for entry. Never leave keys in locks, under the doormat, or hanging inside the letterbox.

# Choosing locks and latches for your doors

Choosing an appropriate lock or latch for each door in the house is crucial for safety and security. But remember that any lock is only as strong as the frame to which it is fitted and the screws you use.

Single-point locks and latches are available in two main types.
• Rim locks are screwed to the inside of the door; they are easy to install but not so secure as they are only held by screws, and could be forced off the door.
• Mortise locks are fitted (mortised) into the door edge; they are more difficult and time-consuming to install, but more secure because the door frame has to be smashed to get past them. A metal reinforcement, called a London bar, can be fitted to the frame beside a mortise lock (see page 87), but this must be ordered to size to fit the exact positioning of the locks on your particular door.

Multi-point locking systems (see page 84) can secure a door along its full height. Modern uPVC double-glazed doors are usually supplied with a secure multi-point locking system.

Always make sure that a door frame is sound, free from rot and securely fixed in place before you fit a lock to it or it will be too easy to force the door by breaking the frame or pushing the fixing screws out of their holes.

## Back doors

A deadlock is a lock with a bolt that can be opened only with a key. This type of lock is essential for side and back doors, because these doors are often glazed and in secluded positions, where passers-by are less likely to notice a burglar breaking the glass and reaching in to open the latch from inside.

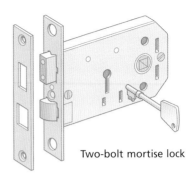

Two-bolt mortise lock

Two-bolt mortise lock The two-bolt mortise lock is also called a mortise sashlock. The latch is operated by handles on both sides of the door and the bolt can be operated only by the key. Choose one with five levers for good security (or buy an upgrader unit) and use only locks manufactured to British Standard BS3621. Narrow models are available for doors with narrow stiles. Use with rack bolts at top and bottom of the door. Take the dimensions of the old lock when buying a new one, as sizes vary according to make.

Two-bolt rim lock This screws to the inside face of the door. It is simple to install but easy to tamper with. Cheaper one, two and three-lever actions are unsuitable as the sole lock for external doors. Fit additional bolts at top and bottom.

## Front doors

If you have glass in your front door, buy a deadlocking cylinder rimlock. This becomes unmovable if you turn the key when you leave the house, so that a burglar will not be able to reach in through a broken pane of glass to open the door.

Cylinder rim lock The lock is fitted to the inner face of the door. The latch is turned back by a key from the outside and by a handle from the inside. A 'snib' (knob) holds the latch in place – either out or in. This is less secure than a deadlocking cylinder rim lock. When choosing the lock, look for one made to British Standards Institution BS3621. To keep the door locked when you are indoors, choose a model with a lockable handle, so that it can be locked from the inside as well as the outside. But ensure that a key is kept near the door in case of fire. Use with a mortise deadlock for extra security.

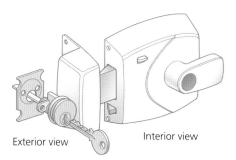

Exterior view          Interior view

**Deadlocking cylinder rim lock** (above) The lock is fitted to the inner face of the door. When the key is turned in the lock, the bolt cannot be forced back. On some models the main bolt automatically deadlocks when the door is closed. Bolts on standard locks are about 14mm; bolts on high-security designs are 20mm or more. A locking handle on the inside prevents an intruder from opening the door after breaking a glass panel. Use only locks manufactured to BS3621. A BSEN1303 grade 5 cylinder provides anti-drill and pick resistance. Some models incorporate a lock check indicator so you can see if the door is deadlocked. Use with a mortise deadlock for added security.

**Latchbolt** Instead of a rim lock, a latchbolt (also called a locking latch) can be fitted. This has a bolt and a latch. The latch is operated by a handle on the inside while the bolt is key-operated from either side.

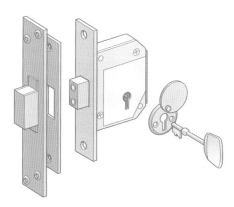

**Mortise deadlock** (above) The bolt cannot be turned back without using the key. The key operates levers, and the more levers there are, the harder the lock is to pick. A five or seven-lever lock with a box type striking plate gives the best security. Use with a rim lock for frequent comings and goings. Cutting a mortise into a door will weaken it a little, so if you have a front door that is less than 45mm thick ask for a thin-pattern mortise lock.

## Patio doors and French windows

Small security locks can be mounted on the inside of a wood or metal patio door. They operate a bolt which engages in a hole in the other door. For maximum security, fit locks at both top and bottom of the door. This is particularly advisable for old aluminium-framed patio doors which can sometimes be jemmied out of the sliding track and lifted out of the frame.

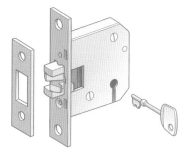

**Clawbolt deadlock** A pair of claws lock into the striking plate, and can only be operated by a key. The lock is mortised into the door's stile. Suitable for sliding patio doors made of wood. Metal patio doors usually come with their own lock.

**Casement bolt (espagnolette bolt)** This is the traditional way to lock French windows. A full length bolt, operated by a central handle, shoots into the frame at top and bottom. For security it should be used in conjunction with rack bolts (see page 84) at the top and bottom.

## Internal doors

Internal doors are best not locked when a house is empty. Once a thief is inside he will usually not be deterred by locked doors unless they are very strong.

When the house is occupied, ground floor doors could be locked at night. A burglar trying to get from, say, the living room to the rest of the house will probably make so much noise that he will wake the occupants. For this purpose, fit a two-bolt mortise lock (page 82), as you would for a back or side door; handles on both sides of the door will be necessary for normal use in the daytime. There are now 'lift-and-lock' sashlocks available that allow the door to be locked and unlocked from the inside simply by lifting or depressing the handle; no key is required.

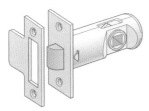

**Mortise latch** This is suitable only for keeping doors closed; it cannot be locked. A small model can be inserted in a circular hole. Bathroom doors normally require a latch with a 'snib', a simple locking device that can be turned from the inside for privacy. A screw slot on the outside of the door can be used to open the latch in an emergency.

# Additional devices for door security

Door chains, hinge bolts and various other supplementary locking devices can be fitted to further enhance either the security of external doors or the safety of the occupants.

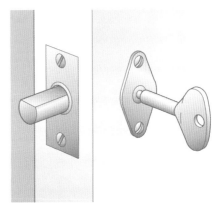

**Rack bolts** With every external door it is advisable to fit rack bolts to prevent forcing. The bolts are mortised into the opening edge of the door. Fit two to each door – one at the top and one at the bottom.

Rack bolts are an alternative method of locking a front door at night when the house is occupied. If the glass is broken it

## MULTI-LOCKING SYSTEMS FOR SECLUDED DOORS

External doors that are not overlooked are especially vulnerable because attempts by an intruder to gain entrance are unlikely to be spotted. To counter this, a multi-point locking system is advisable. This locking system can be used on doors 30–47mm thick, made of uPVC, composite material, timber or aluminium. Locking mechanisms can be fitted along the full length of the door. The high-security hookbolts are activated by pulling the door handle up, and retracted by pulling the handle down. The door cannot be locked until all the bolts are thrown, and turning the key will deadlock all locking points as well as the latch bolt.

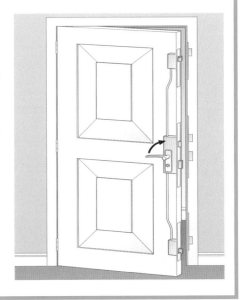

is hard to see where the bolts are fitted. Even if the holes are found, a fluted key is needed to undo them.

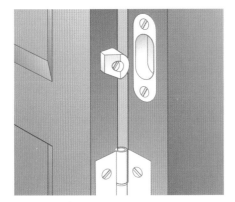

**Hinge bolts** It is possible to unhinge a door by using a jemmy on the hinge side. To prevent this, fit hinge bolts – two per door – about 75mm away from the hinges.

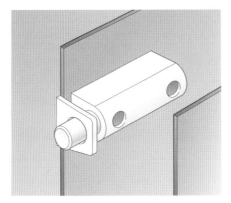

**Self-locking bolts** Where a door is too thin to house a rack bolt without being weakened, fit a surface mounted, self-locking bolt. It is merely screwed in place; when fitted, all screws are concealed. Pushing the bolt end slides it into the locked position, where it deadlocks and cannot be moved without using a key.

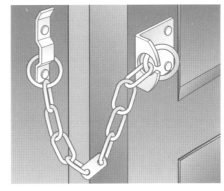

**Door chains** To prevent an intruder forcing his way in after ringing the doorbell, fit a chain to the front door. It allows the door to be opened just far enough to speak to a caller, but the door has to be shut again before the chain can be released to allow entry.

The strength of the device depends entirely on how well the chain is anchored to door and frame, so use the longest and heaviest-gauge screws possible.

Various patterns are available, including a simple chain, a chain combined with a sliding bolt, a chain which can be unlocked from the outside with a key, and a chain with an in-built alarm, which is triggered by an attempt to enter.

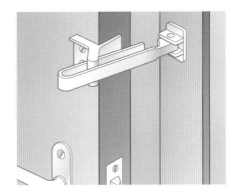

**Door limiter** A more substantial version of a door chain is a door limiter, with a sliding bar replacing the chain. When in place, the bar engages with the retaining part of the unit, restricting the opening of the door. The door has to be closed and the bar swung away before it can be fully opened.

# Adding security bolts to doors

Although most door locks are secure, you may feel the need for added safety – in which case, security bolts may be your best choice.

## Fitting a rack bolt

Tools *Pencil; drill and bits (sizes according to the manufacturer's instructions); pliers; 19mm chisel; screwdriver; try square.*

Materials *Rack bolt.*

**1** Mark a central point on the edge of the door where you want to fit the bolt. Use a try square and pencil to continue the mark onto the inner face of the door.

### SAFETY SPYHOLES

A simple way to improve your personal safety at home is to fit a spyhole in your front door. These wide-angled viewers enable you to see who is calling before you open the door. They work best in unglazed doors where you can look out without being seen, but can be fitted in any door where there is a central bar that you can drill through. If you try to fit one in the side rail of the door, close to the locks, you may find that you cannot comfortably look through it.

**2** Drill a hole into the edge of the door to the diameter and depth of the body of the bolt.

**3** Wind out the bolt and push it into the hole. Mark round the faceplate, withdraw the bolt with pliers and cut a shallow recess for the faceplate with a chisel.

**4** Hold the bolt flush with the face of the door and mark the spot for the key. Drill a hole (see the manufacturer's instructions for the size) through the inside face of the door only.

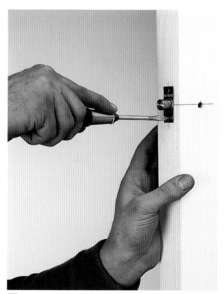

**5** Push the bolt back into the door and screw the faceplate to the edge of the door. Check that the bolt operates correctly. If necessary, enlarge the keyhole.

**6** Screw the keyhole plate to the inside of the door.

**7** Close the door and wind out the bolt to mark the door jamb. There is usually a pimple on the end of the bolt to mark the wood.

**8** Open the door and drill a hole to the required depth at the mark. Check that the bolt will go smoothly into this hole.

**9** Hold the cover plate over the hole, draw around it, cut out a shallow recess and screw the cover plate in place. Check the operation of the bolt and make any necessary adjustments.

## Fitting hinge bolts

**Tools** *Pencil; drill and bits (see instructions for size); mallet; chisel; screwdriver.*

**Materials** *A pair of hinge bolts.*

**1** Open the door fully and mark the centre of the door edge about 75mm away from the hinges at the top and the bottom.

**2** Drill a hole into the door edge to the diameter and depth given in the maker's instructions. Wrap coloured adhesive tape round the bit as a depth guide.

**3** Push the bolt into the hole. Partially close the door so that the bolt marks the frame.

**4** At this spot, drill a hole into the frame to the depth of the protruding bolt, plus a little more for clearance. Check that the door shuts easily. If necessary, enlarge the hole.

**5** Open the door and hold the cover plate over the hole. Mark the edge of the plate with a pencil and chisel out a recess so the plate lies flush with the frame.
Fix the plate in place with the screws provided.

---

### REINFORCING A DOOR LATCH OR LOCK

Doors secured with a rim lock or cylinder latch are quite easily forced: a heavy blow drives the latch against the staple, which is held in place by just a couple of screws, shearing it away from the inside face of the frame and allowing an intruder to get in. A London bar (right) is designed to prevent this; it consists of a long steel bar shaped to fit tightly over the staple and is fixed with screws all the way down the inside face of the frame.

You can also strengthen doors and frames around locks and hinges with so-called partnered reinforcements. These consist of two metal strips, joined together by bolts which pass right through the door or frame. For example, a mortise lock can be protected with a pair of strips bolted through the frame on either side of the keep plate, and by a further pair on the door, sandwiching the lock.

# Cylinder door lock

Nearly every front door is fitted with this type of lock. It has an ingenious mechanism, and one that is easy to put right if the familiar flat key fails to turn. For maximum security, you should fit a five or seven lever mortise deadlock, too.

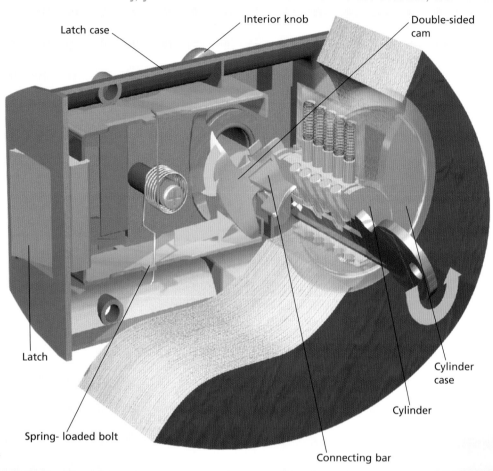

Latch case

Interior knob

Double-sided cam

Latch

Spring- loaded bolt

Connecting bar

Cylinder

Cylinder case

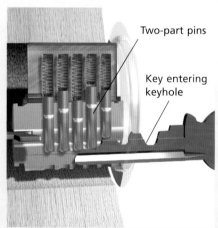

Two-part pins

Key entering keyhole

**1** As the key is pushed into the keyhole, its notched edge pushes up a series of two-part pins, the ends of which are held against each other by springs.

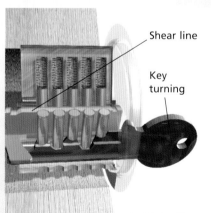

Shear line

Key turning

**2** When the key is fully in, the breaks in the tops of the pins will all coincide with the shear line between the case and cylinder, allowing the cylinder to turn with the key.

**3** The connecting bar sticking out from the end of the cylinder turns a double-sided cam, which operates a spring-loaded bolt to depress the latch.

**4** Releasing the key reverses the sequence: the spring-loaded bolt pushes the latch out; the cam, connecting bar and cylinder turn; and the ends of the pins line up.

**5** The interior knob also operates a double-sided cam to push on the spring-loaded bolt and depress the latch into its case, allowing the door to be opened.

## IF THE KEY STICKS

If you find that you cannot turn the key in the lock or it is difficult to remove once you have opened the door, the cylinder is probably worn. In time, the ends of the pins become worn, making it increasingly difficult to turn the key. However, as long as the interior knob is not operated by a key, you can buy just a replacement cylinder (see right), together with new keys.

# Replacing a cylinder

**1** Remove the latch case on the inside of the door and undo the two screw-headed bolts securing the cylinder to the mounting plate. Use the other hand to support the lock on the outside of the door, so that it does not fall out.

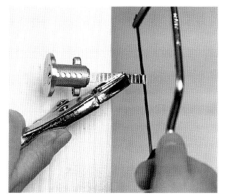

**2** Hold the connecting bar of the replacement cylinder with an adjustable wrench or pliers and cut with a junior hacksaw to same length as that on old cylinder. File the end smooth.

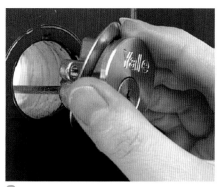

**3** Slide the replacement cylinder into place and connect it to the mounting plate with the bolts, checking that the maker's name on the lock face stays upright as you tighten the bolts. Refit the latch case and make sure the new key turns smoothly to operate the lock.

# Mortise door lock

A mortise deadlock is commonly used as a second lock on a front door that already has a cylinder lock. The more levers a mortise lock has, the harder it is to pick. Choose a lock with a minimum of five levers (shown below). One with seven is better still.

**1** A mortise key has a series of notches. When the key is inserted into the keyhole and turned, these notches align with the levers inside the lock casing, which are held in place by springs.

**2** As the key is turned, the notches raise each lever to the height of its gate. Only at this position can the stump pass the gate, freeing the bolt.

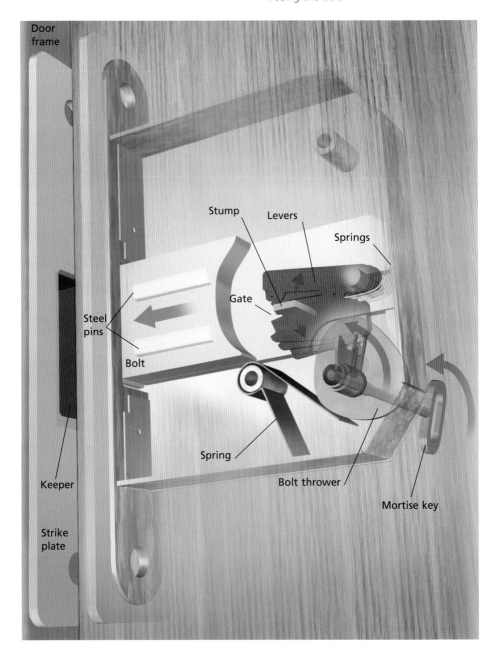

Door frame

Stump

Levers

Springs

Gate

Steel pins

Bolt

Spring

Bolt thrower

Mortise key

Keeper

Strike plate

**3** The key also turns the bolt thrower, which is kept in place by a spring. The bolt thrower has a ridge (shown in blue), which pushes the bolt out into the strike plate and keeper. The springs push the levers back down into a locked position when the bolt is fully extended. The door is now deadlocked.

**4** Steel pins embedded in the bolt roll under a hacksaw blade, making it impossible to saw through the bolt. The casing is made of drill-resistant hardened steel. The keeper in the door frame is a steel box, which prevents an intruder forcing the bolt back into the lock.

**5** To unlock the door, the key is turned in the opposite direction. The notches on the key raise the levers to free the bolt, which is moved back towards the lock by the bolt thrower.

## Strength and security

A lock is only as strong as the door and frame in which it is fitted. Replace fragile wood before fitting new locks. Also, one lock may not be enough to secure against determined force. Fit a mortise lock and a cylinder lock at different heights on the door. This spreads the load of any blows to the door.

Buy only locks that conform to British Standard BS 3621.

### KEY COMBINATIONS

The key is a solid piece of metal with a bow at one end, which can be hooked onto a key ring. At the other end of the shank ❷ is the shoulder ❸, which prevents the key from sliding right through the keyhole. The post ❹ and bit ❺ are the parts that fit inside the lock. Each notch ❻ in the bit can be cut to one of seven different positions. There will be five notches in a key for a five-lever lock (shown above). Despite security restrictions on the relative position and depth of notches, a five-lever lock will have more than 1000 possible combinations.

## Replacing a mortise lock

**1** Open the door to expose the bolt and the strike plate. Unscrew the strike plate, then turn the key to operate the bolt.

**2** Remove the key and then slide out the lock by gripping the projecting bolt with pliers and pulling outwards.

**3** Push a matching replacement lock into the door, and secure the lock and strike plate with the screws.

**4** Make sure the new key turns smoothly to operate the lock.

# Choosing security locks for your windows

Windows are the main points of entry for burglars. The most common method of breaking in is to smash the glass and release the catch. Window locks will lock the frames together, make the handle immovable, or restrain the stay arm.

Before buying window locks, make sure they are suitable for your windows. A lock for timber frames will come with woodscrews. Locks for metal windows will have self-tapping screws. Make sure the frames are thick enough to accommodate the device.

## Metal windows

**Locking clamp** A key shoots a bolt from the window into a bracket mounted on the frame.

**Stay bolt** Fits underneath the stay arm. A bolt slides under the stay retainer, preventing the arm from being lifted.

**Cockspur bolt** When the cockspur handle is closed, the case of the bolt is moved up on the fixed frame and locked, preventing the cockspur from opening. Alternatively, a locking cockspur handle can be fitted.

## Sash window locks

**Sash stop** A locking nut screws into a mounting plate on the upper sash to prevent the lower sash from sliding up. They can be positioned a little higher to allow the window to be opened a little for ventilation. Fit one on each side on large windows.

**Sash window** A two-part surface-fitted lock secures the two meeting rails together, in place of the standard interlocking sash catch. A push bolt locks the inner and outer plate together. They are released with a key.

**Dual screw** A long, steel, key-operated screw goes through a barrel in the inner sash into a threaded sleeve in the outer sash. Fit two dual screws if the window is wide.

## Casement window locks

### For locking frames together

**Mortise rack bolt** The lock is mortised into the opening frame, and the bolt slides into a hole in the fixed frame. They are suitable only for windows at least 35mm thick. More difficult to install than a surface-fitting lock, however it gives excellent security. Fit close to the centre of the opening edge. On large windows, fit a mortise rack bolt at each end of the opening edge.

### For locking the handle and stay

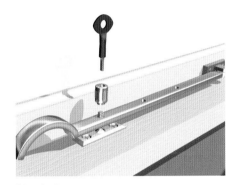

**Stay lock** Replaces the pegs that secure the stay when closed. The peg is threaded and is locked by screwing on a key-operated nut. Ventilation locks allow the window to be locked closed or slightly open: the peg locates in a short sliding bar fixed to the casement, so the position can be adjusted.

**Swing-bar lock** A C-shaped bar fixed to the casement swings over a locking plate on the frame to stop the window from opening. The bar can be locked with a mechanical key.

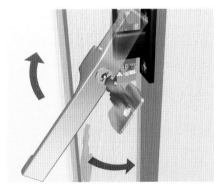

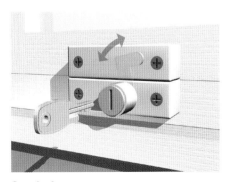

**Cam lock** A key turns a cam, or notched rotating shaft, into the second part of the lock, fixed to the frame, securing the two components together.

**Locking handle** A new handle with a lock replaces the existing cockspur handle. Once locked, it cannot be opened without the key. Make sure you buy the correct right-hand or left-hand type for your window. Some types allow the window to be locked slightly ajar for ventilation. Alternatively, a blocking bolt can be fitted to the fixed frame that prevents the cockspur handle from moving, if it is on the frame surface. The bolt is retracted with the key.

# Fitting locks to windows

Most locks come with clear fitting instructions. These are three of the most common and effective window locks to fit yourself.

## Casement window lock

Surface-mounted locks are easy to fit to casement windows, provided that the surfaces of the fixed frame and the opening casement are at right angles to each other.
• If the fixed frame is tapered, wood may have to be chiselled so the lock fits against the opening frame. Some locks are supplied with a wedge to get over this problem.

• For large windows, or for extra security, fit two locks on each frame, at top and bottom. They will withstand a jemmy attack better than a single lock.

• The technique shown below is for a swing-bar lock, but other models are installed in a similar way.

Tools *Pencil; drill and twist bits; bradawl; screwdriver. Perhaps a small chisel.*

Materials *One or two window locks, depending on size of window.*

**1** Open the window and position the locking plate on the frame, 1mm from the edge. Make sure it is straight, mark the position of the holes with a bradawl and screw the plate in place.

**2** Close the window and position the body of the lock behind the locking plate. Fix one screw, check the operation of the lock, then drive in the second screw.

## Metal-framed window lock

Locks are fitted to a steel or aluminium window frame with self-tapping screws, which should be supplied with the lock. To drill a pilot hole in the frame, use a high-speed-steel (HSS) twist bit. Most locks come with instructions giving the drill size.

If in doubt, make the hole the same diameter as the 'core' of the screw, not the shank. Use a bit that is too small rather than too big.

Tools *Bradawl or ball-point pen; electric drill; HSS twist bits; screwdriver.*

Materials *Window lock with self-tapping screws.*

**1** Hold the lock in position and mark the screw hole with a bradawl or ball-point pen.

**2** Drill a pilot hole just through the metal. Provided the bit is sharp, it should not skid on the metal.

**3** Screw the lock to the frame. If the screw hole is too tight, re-drill the hole one size bigger.

## Dual screw sash window lock

A dual screw is a very secure locking device for a sash window, but it is not practical if the window is opened frequently.

**Before you start** If the window is opened often, use a surface-fitted bolt (see page 92). For large windows, fit two locks, one at each end of the centre meeting rail.
 Dual screws vary in design. Some have barrels for both inner and outer frames, other have a lockplate for the outer frame.

**Tools** *Drill and auger bit the width of the lock barrel; hammer and piece of wood, or a large screwdriver (depending on the model). Perhaps a small screwdriver, small twist bit and chisel (depending on model).*

**Materials** *One or two dual screws.*

---

### SAFETY AND SECURITY

**Laminated glass**
Particular windows in a house may be at risk from burglars. They may be ground-floor windows hidden from the neighbours, or they may be upstairs windows that are accessible from an extension roof, a drainpipe or a tree. Fitting laminated glass would add greatly to the security. It consists of a sandwich of glass with a clear plastic film between. Although the glass may be cracked by a blow, the plastic will resist efforts to break through. Do not use wired glass, because it has little security value.

**Plastic windows**
An increasing number of plastic windows are being used in houses, and they can pose a security problem. Most manufacturers of security devices do not recommend them for plastic windows because a thin plastic section offers no grip for screws. If a plastic window frame is known to have a timber inner frame, security devices suitable for a wooden frame can be used. If there are steel inserts within the plastic section, self-tapping screws could be used, as for metal frames. But locks cannot be fitted to hollow sections of windows filled with rigid foam. The ideal solution is to consult the installer of your windows at the time they are being made.

**1** Drill through the inner meeting rail and on into the outer meeting rail to a depth of 15mm. Wind some tape around the bit as a guide to the depth of the hole. Take care not to catch the edge of the glass.

**2** Tap the longer barrel into the inner meeting rail, using a hammer and a piece of wood to protect it from being damaged. Squeeze it into the frame using a G-cramp if the frame is old and the glass liable to shatter.

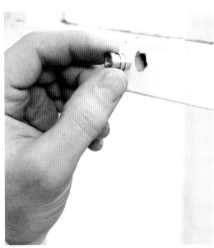

**3** Reverse the sashes. Tap the shorter barrel into the outer meeting rail. Alternatively, fit the locking plate to the outer meeting rail. If the sashes clash as they pass, recess the plate with a chisel.

**4** Close the window and screw the bolt into the barrel with the key. Trim the bolt with a hacksaw if it is too long.

# Repairing a broken window

A cracked or broken window makes your home an easier target for burglars. It should be repaired with safety glass – 400 children a year suffer broken-glass-related injuries.

---

## PROTECTION FROM CUTS

Always wear thick leather shoes when removing a broken pane or cutting glass, in case a jagged piece falls on your foot. Protect your hands with heavy gloves and eyes with safety spectacles or goggles.

---

### Tape a cracked pane
If glass is cracked but intact, crisscross the pane with masking tape to lessen the risk of flying shards when you break it, then use a hacking knife to remove the putty. Break the pane from inside with a hammer and a block of wood. Lift out large shards first, then chip out and remove the smaller pieces.

### Emergency cover
Seal a cracked pane temporarily with transparent waterproof glazing tape, applied to the outside. If the pane is smashed, cover the whole window with heavy-gauge polythene secured by timber battens nailed round the frame.

If good security is vital, nail a sheet of plywood across the window frame until you can replace the glass.

## The best glass for the job

### Light and privacy
Choose patterned (obscured) glass where you need to let light in but at the same time retain your privacy – the windows in bathrooms or glazed front doors, for example.

### Safe and secure
Use safety glass in doors and for any fixed panes prone to impact damage.

**Toughened glass** shatters into harmless granules if broken. It must be ordered to size because it cannot be cut or drilled once it has been made.

Laminated glass, which can be cut in the usual way, is made of two layers of glass sandwiching a plastic interlayer. It cracks but doesn't fragment because the interlayer holds the pieces together. It also makes good security glazing.

Safety wired glass is often used in fire doors to reduce the rate of spread of fire. It should not be confused with ordinary wired glass, which has little security value.

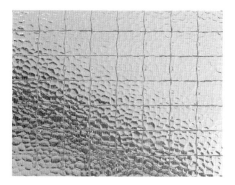

### Safety glass is essential

If you are carrying out improvements or alterations to your home that involve the installation of new glazed doors and windows, you must use safety glass in areas that are prone to impact damage to comply with the Building Regulations. For full details of where it must be fitted, contact your local authority Building Control office or ask a glass merchant.

### Allow for escape from fire

Include an opening casement big enough to act as a fire escape when choosing new windows, especially for upstairs rooms. Fixed double-glazed panes are very difficult to break in an emergency. Keep the keys to window locks to hand in each room and make sure everyone knows where they are.

## BUILDING REGULATIONS

If you are fitting replacement windows, certain doors or roof lights to your home, there are two ways to ensure compliance with relevant regulations:
• Employ a contractor or installer who is registered under the FENSA self-certification scheme;
• Arrange for Building Regulations approval. This will consider such things as structure, means of escape in a fire, ventilation and access.
In addition to Building Regulations approval, you may need planning permission or conservation area consent.

### Cover with safety film

You can make conventional glass in high-risk areas safer by covering it on the inside with a special, strong, self-adhesive plastic film that holds it together if broken.

### Reduce glare and fading

Prevent soft furnishings, rugs and paintings in sunny rooms from fading by installing laminated glass. The plastic interlayer filters out most of the sun's ultraviolet rays, which cause the damage.

Cut the heat build-up in a south-facing conservatory by using tinted, coated solar control glass or low-emissivity glass (below).

# Doorbell and entry system

Whereas a doorbell is a simple circuit between a button at the door and a chime in the house, an entry system consists of a camera, microphone and speaker at the door, and a screen and telephone-type handset inside.

**1** When a visitor presses the call button, the camera and light are turned on. At the same time, a buzzer sounds inside the property and the monitor displays the image from the camera.

**2** When the occupant lifts the handset a two-way audio connection is established between the microphone and speaker at the door and the handset through a wire. The monitor displays the moving picture taken by the camera.

**3** To admit the visitor, the entry button is pressed. This activates a solenoid release catch, which pulls back a catch in the door lock mortise allowing the door to open.

## FAULT DIAGNOSIS

It is not possible to repair a video entry system yourself. Use this panel to help diagnose the problem before consulting a qualified repairer.

**No picture**
No power to camera
Camera failed
Poor connection to camera
No power to monitor

**No sound**
No connection to microphone

**Open button does not work**
No connection to solenoid release catch

**Doorbell faults**
If a standard doorbell stops working, it is easier to fix. Consider the following likely causes:

Flat battery – replace
Faulty bell-push – replace
Bad connection in bell wire – replace wire between bell-push and bell
Jammed chimes – reposition bars

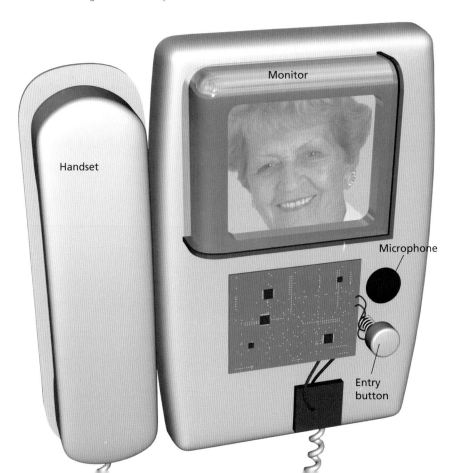

Monitor

Handset

Microphone

Entry button

## The exterior unit

Positioned on an exterior wall, this part of an entry system consists of the light, camera, speaker, call button and microphone, and solenoid release catch that is operated automatically from within the house to unlock the door.

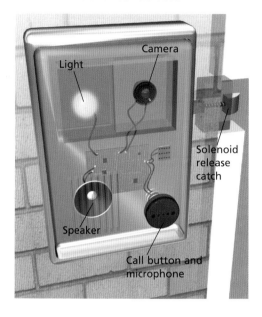

## A simple doorbell

A basic door chime consists of a switch, a power supply and a bell. When the button is pushed, metal contacts ❷ meet and form a circuit between the power supply ❸ and a solenoid ❹. This pushes a rod ❺ towards a chime bar ❻. When the circuit is broken, the magnet releases the bar. A spring ❼ forces it to bounce back and hit the second chime ❽, making the second tone of the bell. Other systems use an electromagnet to pull a hammer back, at which point the circuit is broken and the hammer hits a bell.

## Fixing a doorbell wire

**1** If the doorbell is mains powered, turn off the power first. If it is battery powered, remove the bell unit cover and take out the batteries. Then unscrew the bell push from the door frame. Remove the terminal screws retaining the old wire and connect a new length of wire. You may have to route the cable through a hole in the door frame first. Replace the bell push.

**2** Cut the new wire to the length of the old one. Make a note of the position of the connections, then remove the old wire from the bell unit and attach the new wires to the terminals. Fix the new wire to the wall and door frame. If the bell is mains powered, replace the cover and turn on the mains power. Otherwise, replace the batteries and reattach the cover. Then test the bell push.

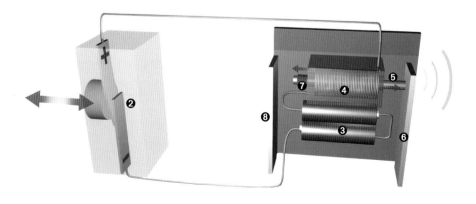

# Choosing a burglar alarm

The simplest type of burglar alarm has detectors built into door and window frames that sense when the door or window is opened and sound a siren or bell. The more complex systems combine these sensors with infra-red detectors, and may also call an emergency telephone number when an intruder is detected.

Most thieves are likely to be deterred by locks on windows and doors, but you may decide to install an alarm system as an extra defence against a burglar who tries to force his way in. A noisy alarm may deter him from entering the house, or greatly reduce the time he stays there.

Before buying a system, check that the alarm is loud enough. Anything below 95 decibels has little effect and cannot be heard over any distance. Most alarms sound for about 20 minutes and then reset to avoid nuisance to neighbours. Notify your local police and your neighbours that an alarm has been fitted, and give a trusted neighbour a spare key to the system or the code number. Ensure that the alarm you choose has a 'closed' electrical circuit. This means that when the system is turned on the circuit is completed. If there is any interference – such as the wires being cut – the alarm will go off.

A system has three main components: the switches; the control; and the alarm. A valuable addition to this is a panic button, which can be used to trigger the alarm at any time. Some burglar-alarm systems are designed for DIY installation, others need to be professionally fitted.

## Whole-house systems

**Control unit** The 'brain' of the system is the control unit, which receives signals from the switches and sends an electric current to activate the alarm. The system is turned on or off with a key or a push-button panel to which a code number is first keyed in. In many systems, the control unit can also be used to alarm specific zones, such as upstairs or downstairs.

Connected with the control unit will be some form of power supply, either mains or battery. In some models mains power will feed the system under normal conditions, but if the power is cut off, a battery will take over. The battery is automatically recharged when power is restored. The control unit may also dial a telephone number to notify a security company or nominated neighbour of illegal entry.

**Passive infra-red (PIR) motion detectors** These are small units, fitted at ceiling height, which sense movement through changes of temperature within their field of detection. Even if a person moves very slowly across a room, the detectors will pick up his or her body heat.

**Magnetic door and window contacts** A magnetic switch can be fitted to a door or window that opens. One part is secured to the frame, the other to the door or casement. When the door or window is opened, the circuit is broken and the alarm system is triggered.

**External alarm** The alarm has a bell or siren that should be loud enough to frighten off potential intruders and alert neighbours.

## STAY SECURE

Make sure your burglar alarm and locks comply with the Association for Chief Police Officers' (ACPO) standards.

Some external sirens also incorporate a bright, flashing strobe light; others feature flashing LEDs to indicate that the system is active and to add to the visual deterrent.

The external alarm box should be tamper-proof and should contain its own battery, so that it will still sound if the cable to it is cut.

**Panic button** A manually operated switch can be fitted as a panic button – at the bedside or by the front door. It is usually wired so that it will trigger the alarm whether or not the rest of the system is switched on. Panic buttons can be very sensitive; the slightest pressure will set off the alarm.

**Wireless systems** A good option for DIY installation can be a wireless system. PIR sensors and magnetic door contacts are all independently battery powered and transmit a radio signal to the control unit when they sense movement; this in turn triggers the alarm. These 'wirefree' systems can be set using a remote key fob switch that doubles as a mobile panic alarm. Some systems offer a repeater unit, which increases the transmission range so that outbuildings may also be protected.

## Essential system maintenance

For it to be effective in an emergency, it is crucial to keep your burglar alarm system in good working order and to check all its elements regularly. Ensure that everyone in the household knows how to use the alarm properly.

### On installation

**Rehearse turning the alarm off.** Make sure everyone in the household can access the control unit and knows how to disable the alarm quickly. Include all key-holders in this routine.

### Once every six months

**Check batteries (if any) in system.** Some control units have back-up batteries – make sure they are fresh or charging properly if rechargeable. Consult the manufacturer's instructions for details. Wireless detectors also run on batteries.

### Once a year

**Have system tested and serviced.** Call the security company which supplied the alarm to arrange to have your system checked.

## Individual alarm devices

**Door alarm** This unit can be fitted to an external door and will sound if the door is opened. It is battery operated, so no wiring is needed. The alarm is turned off with a push-button code that you set yourself, or with a key. A delay switch allows several seconds for you to enter or leave the house without triggering the alarm.

**Shed alarm** This type of self-contained, battery-powered alarm can be fixed in a shed, garage, caravan or greenhouse. It will pick up movement within its field of detection and activate its own alarm.

### REPEATED FALSE ALARMS

If your alarm starts sounding repeatedly it will soon become a neighbourhood nuisance. Check that all protected windows and doors are closed properly and that an open circuit breaker is not causing the problem. If this does not stop the false alarms, have the system checked for faults.

# CCTV systems

Closed circuit television camera (CCTV) systems are a familiar sight in public places, such as railway stations, airports and shopping centres. Now, they are being installed by householders, too, as a crime prevention tool.

Simple closed circuit television camera (CCTV) surveillance systems can be bought fairly cheaply, and you can install them yourself. Visit your local DIY store to see what kind of equipment is available. There is one thing to beware of, however. If you live somewhere remote or in an area of very low crime, a visible CCTV camera may suggest that you have something worth stealing – and a burglar who may not previously have given the house a second glance might change his mind.

## Security when you are away

Some cameras are designed to keep watch on your car or record activity outside your home even while you are out or away. They may be activated by PIR (Passive Infra-red) sensors similar to those found on security lights and only start to record when they detect activity in the camera's field of vision, or they may take still photographs every few seconds to provide a time-lapse recording of what has been going on.

## Why install CCTV?

Before you consider installing CCTV, have in place good basic security – from sturdy locks and security lighting to burglar alarms and even noisy dogs. The reasons people choose CCTV are:
• To watch the area immediately outside their home;
• To deter unwanted visitors;
• To record vandals at work to use as evidence in a court of law.

What effects might CCTV have? If vandals are drunk or high on drugs, they will ignore the cameras or even play to them. A potential intruder will do his best to locate a point of entry out of camera vision – or to disable the camera. But if the camera is just one of a range of security measures,

most opportunist burglars will head for a softer target.

The equipment Most domestic CCTV systems sold in DIY superstores are inexpensive and fairly basic. They come with integrated cameras and lenses – often referred to as 'bullet' cameras – that are sealed so as to be watertight. Their small size makes them ideal for fitting to domestic properties. You can't adjust the lens, but most are set up to film a 72° viewing angle, which is fine for domestic use. They provide a wide general view and can be used to identify an individual standing up to 10m away from the lens. The image can be quite fuzzy – so don't expect to be able to survey a wide area nor for the resolution to be sharp enough to identify someone's face at a distance.

Cameras may be connected to a monitor with cabling (above) or you may choose a wireless system (see opposite). You will also need to decide how to monitor and record the images captured by the camera (see opposite page).

How much detail do you need? The term 'resolution' is used to describe the amount of picture detail in the image produced by the camera. It is expressed as the number of television lines that the camera is capable of producing. For example, a monochrome (black-and-white) bullet camera may be classed as 420 lines (420TVL). The higher the TVL, the better the resolution.

You should be able to read the number plate of a stationary car with a resolution of 380TVL; go below 300TVL and it will become hard even to identify a person's facial features. Picture quality also depends on light and shade levels, so these are only broad guidelines.

Where to site the camera Modern 'bullet' cameras are small and neat enough to be fixed inconspicuously on or under the fascia or soffit boards, where the roof meets the wall. From here, it is quite straightforward to run the cables into the loft. The position affords shelter from wind, rain and excessive sunlight, while the height provides a good view and minimises the risk of vandalism.

**Wireless cameras** These can be fitted in minutes as there are no cables that you have to run back to your TV or monitor. The big disadvantage is that they use a lot of power, with most batteries giving a working time of less than 24 hours, which is also expensive.

## Recording CCTV Images

There are three main ways to record the images from your CCTV set-up.

**Domestic VCR** A video recorder is the simplest and cheapest solution. It will give you eight hours of continuous recording time and can be set up to provide event-only recording, triggered by a movement in the camera's field of vision. However, most domestic videos are slow to start up and there is a danger that you might miss vital footage. You cannot record television programmes when camera input is selected, so it's best to have a dedicated VCR.

**Time-lapse VCR** A slow-moving tape records the camera snapshots at split-second intervals. The time-lapse can be set to give 24, 240 or even 960 hours of recording on standard VCR tapes – the longer the recording time the longer the delay between snapshots.

**Digital video recorder (DVR)** This takes images from the camera, digitises them and stores them on the hard drive of a PC. This system is much more expensive than the others, but is also simpler to install. You don't need to set the DVR to record continually – the better ones have a built-in motion detection system that triggers record mode. You can access the recording of any known time and date almost instantaneously, while the vast storage capacity means no changing of tapes. The system is easy to connect to the internet for remote viewing and playback.

**Dummy cameras** In the same way that you can use a dummy burglar alarm housing fixed to your property's exterior, so you can buy a dummy camera as a simple deterrent to would-be burglars.

## Legal considerations

CCTV cameras must be pointed at your own property only – or you could be accused of spying on other people. If you set up a camera to view areas outside your boundary, then passers-by could quite legitimately complain about being spied on and take action against you. Always ensure that your equipment monitors only the spaces it is intended to and consult with your neighbours if there is a chance that parts of their property may be recorded unintentionally.

The potential invasion of privacy resulting in the use of a CCTV system is covered by Human Rights legislation. Under the terms of the Data Protection Act (1998), you don't need to register a home CCTV system. However, anyone using CCTV must display a sign (above) alerting people to the camera's presence. You must also display a sign that states the purpose of the CCTV surveillance, the person responsible for it, and their contact details. You are only permitted to use the CCTV for the purpose for which is has been installed.

# Fitting an outdoor wall light

To install a light on an outside wall, under a porch or on a patio to improve security, follow the same method as for an inside wall light. Choose a weatherproof light fitting designed for an outside wall.

If the light is on a bracket, not a flush-fitting baseplate, you will need waterproof sealant or a rubber gasket to fit the bracket's base.

It is safest to have the switch indoors. You can take the cables for the light and the switch along the same route over the ceiling and down the indoor surface of the external wall on which you are going to install the light.

At the right height for the wall fitting – about 1.8m above ground level – drill from the back of the chase through the inner and outer leaves of the external wall to make a hole to lead the cable outside. Feed the light cable out through the hole.

Install and connect the junction box and the switch in the same way as for an indoor wall light.

# Adding a spur for a wall light

You can add a security wall light by leading a spur from an existing lighting circuit.

Before you start The wall light may incorporate its own switch; if it does not, you can take the spur in and out of a junction box in the ceiling void and connect the new switch cable there.
• The wall light connections must be in a heat-resisting enclosure, so you may need to fit a metal mounting box in the wall.
• If the base of the light fitting is too small to conceal a square box, use a slim architrave mounting box.
• Choose a light that has been wired with an earth conductor or is double-insulated (marked ▣).

Tools *Suitable tools for preparing the route; insulated screwdrivers; sharp knife; wire cutters and strippers; pliers. Perhaps a circuit tester.*

Materials *Wall light; 1mm two-core-and-earth cable; green-and-yellow earth sleeving; metal mounting box, slim architrave box or round dry-lining box; short length of green-and-yellow-insulated earth conductor; connector block with three pairs of terminals (cut from a strip). Perhaps a three-terminal junction box for connecting the spur. For a separate switch, four-terminal junction box; red plastic sleeving; two-gang light switch.*

## Wiring to a wall light

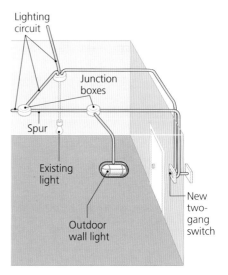

Lighting circuit

Junction boxes

Spur

Existing light

Outdoor wall light

New two-gang switch

Preparation Turn off the power at the main switch in the consumer unit, and remove the fuse or switch off the MCB protecting the circuit you will be working on. Prepare the route for the spur cable. You will need to lead it above the ceiling from a convenient spot on the lighting circuit to a point immediately above the wall-light position, and then down the wall.

The wall light should be about 1.8m above floor level. Make a recess there for the mounting box or slim architrave box.

If the wall light incorporates a switch, lead the spur cable route above the ceiling to a spot halfway between the wall-light position and the switch position and fit the four-way junction box there. Continue the cable run from there to the wall-light position and run another cable from the junction box to a point directly above the switch. You will probably be able to complete the route by enlarging the recess in the plaster leading down the wall to the existing switch. Take great care not to damage the existing switch cable. Unscrew and disconnect the switch. You can use the single mounting box already fitted and fit a two-gang switch over it when you are ready to make the connections.

**1** Lay the spur cable along the route from the circuit either to the wall-light position or to the junction-box position, and from there to the wall-light position and also to the switch position if necessary. Secure the cable along the route.

**2** At the wall light, feed the cable into its mounting box. If you are fitting a switch, feed the switch cable into its mounting box.

**3** Prepare the new cable ends for connection. If you are fitting a switch, slide a piece of brown sleeving on the switch cable's blue core at each end.

**4** Connect the spur to the lighting circuit.

## Light on a base plate

**1** Hold the baseplate of the light fitting against the wall and probe with a bradawl through the fixing holes to mark drilling spots on the wall. Drill holes at the marks and insert wallplugs in them.

**2** Feed the cable through the baseplate and screw the plate to the wall. Prepare the cable for connection.

**3** Connect the brown and blue cores to the terminals of the lampholder; it does not matter which core goes to which terminal. Connect the green-and-yellow sleeved earth core to the terminal marked E or ⏚.

## Light on a bracket

**1** If your light is on a bracket, not a baseplate, you cannot reach the lampholder. Flex will have been connected to it already and the flex end will stick out from the bracket. Prepare the flex cores and connect them to a terminal block.

At the terminals on the opposite side of the block, connect the cores of the light cable. Link brown to brown, blue to blue and earth to earth.

Coat the rim of the bracket's baseplate with sealant, or fit a rubber gasket.

**2** Screw the light fitting into the drilled and plugged holes. Make sure that any sealant or gasket is squeezed tight against the wall to make a weatherproof seal.

## Fitting an outside switch

If you want a switch out of doors as well as inside for the new light, use a two-way sealed splashproof design. Put it on the outside wall back to back with a two-way indoor switch. You will need a short length of three-core-and-earth lighting cable for the connection between the two switches. Drill a hole between the switches and feed the three-core-and-earth cable through it. Connect the cable.

# Choosing time controls for security

**A dark, silent house can arouse the interest of burglars. If you make the house appear occupied, a prowler is likely to move on to an easier target.**

Voices, music and lights after dark can suggest you are in – but only if used with discretion; a single light in the hall left on all evening or a radio playing all day are unlikely to be convincing. The illusion that you are in is best given by a change in the house – music stopping or a light going off in one room and on in another. Sockets and switches operated by timers help to achieve this. Some sophisticated controls will memorise your pattern of light use and reproduce it.

**Sensor lamps** and light sensor switches automatically switch a low-energy bulb on and off at sunset and sunrise; the lamp has a 15,000 hour life. Alternatively, a light sensor switch can be used with tungsten lighting or fluorescent or low-energy fittings. The switch is controlled by a light-sensitive photocell that activates it when daylight fades. The switch-off time is set at one to eight hours after the light comes on.

**Automatic outdoor light** An infra-red sensor activates the light when anyone – visitor or burglar – comes within its field of vision. The sensor can be incorporated in either the light or a separate unit operating a number of lights. Once on, the light shines for a period chosen by the user.

**Light-switch timers**
Time-controlled light switches are connected to the lighting circuit in place of normal switches and are wired in the same way. Some will switch on and off many times. Others switch on only once – at dusk – so there is no danger of the light shining in the daytime because a power cut has interfered with the setting.

**Programmable switch** Digitally controlled, these switches offer a sophisticated combination of on/off switching and are programmable to come on at different times during the week. Features may include light sensor settings and an override. Most can only be used with tungsten lighting, but others have been adapted to use low-voltage or fluorescent lights.

**Plug-in timers** A plug-in timer will control any appliance that plugs into a 13amp socket outlet – a radio or a lamp – to give the impression that the house is occupied. Set the required programme on the timer, plug it into a switched-on outlet, plug the appliance into the timer and switch on the appliance. It will not actually come on until the programmed time. You can override the set programme manually. There are 24-hour and seven-day timers. They vary in the number of times they will switch on and off, and in the shortest possible 'on' period.

**24-hour timer** Some plug-in timers allow you to design a pattern of switching on and off over a 24-hour period. Some models allow up to 48 changes in a day. Markers on a dial trigger the timer to switch on or off as the dial turns. The shortest 'on' period is usually 15–30 minutes. The pattern will be repeated every day until it is switched off or the markers are changed.

**Seven-day timer**
These work in the same way as 24-hour timers, but switching patterns can be varied from day to day over a period of seven days; some will allow up to 84 switchings per week. The on/off pattern will then be repeated each week until altered. The minimum period for which it can be switched on is two hours.

**Electronic digital timer** These offer a number of setting programmes and can allow up to 84 switchings a week. A random setting will switch lights or a radio on or off during the power-on period. It can be used as a daily or weekly timer and will repeat programmes automatically.

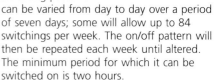

# Security lighting

A PIR (passive infra-red) detector provides the trigger to turn on security lights, which have a range of uses, from illuminating domestic entry ways to providing illumination for security cameras.

**1** When a person moves within the field of view of the PIR detector, the infra-red radiation given off by their body hits two sensors (see burglar alarms, page 100).

**2** The signal from the PIR detector is sent through an amplifier and then activates a switch. This switch completes the larger circuit that incorporates the power source and light bulb, causing the light to switch on.

**3** A dusk sensitivity screw determines when it is dark enough for the PIR detector to operate, while a timer screw determines how long the light bulb stays on. On some models, a PV solar cell charges a battery during the day, which then provides power for the light during the night.

## CHANGING THE BULB

Turn off the power to the unit and allow it to cool. Open the glass and replace the bulb with the correct part. Never touch the surface of a halogen bulb – use a clean, dry cloth to hold it.

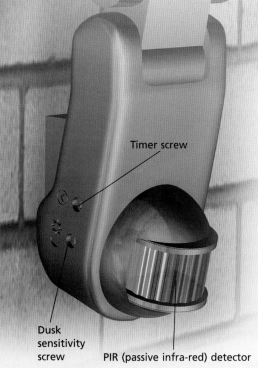

Reflector

Light bulb

Glass cover

Timer screw

Dusk sensitivity screw

PIR (passive infra-red) detector

# Property marking

**An effective way to put thieves off stealing your property is to clearly identify it as belonging to you. This makes it difficult to sell or pass on, and possibly even valueless to a thief.**

Marking your property is a simple way to protect your possessions and also makes it easier for the police to trace and return stolen property to you. It involves using a clear identification mark, which either cannot be erased easily or is invisible until revealed under ultraviolet light. Put stickers on your windows (available from the police) alerting potential burglars that your property is marked and you may deter them from trying to gain entry.

Mark your belongings with your house number and postcode and remember to cross out the markings and re-do them if you move house.

## Marking methods

**Permanent marking** Many items can be engraved or 'punched' with your house number and postcode and permanent marketing kits can be bought from DIY stores. An electric engraver with a fine point is used with a template or stencil to keep the lettering neat and tidy.

Punching – a good option for bicycles, mowers and other sturdy metal items – is done using a hammer and a set of punches bearing numbers and letters. Do not punch aluminium, which is soft and easily damaged.

Alternatively, you can simply scratch identifying marks onto items with something sharp, such as a bradawl or craft knife. This method will not look very neat, but may be appropriate if the mark is out

of sight or on an item where appearance does not matter. Take great care not to injure yourself with the tool you choose to use for the job.

**Invisible marking** A good option for antiques and precious items that would be devalued by permanent marking. Recovered stolen property is normally checked by the police with an ultra-violet (UV) lamp (below), so use a special UV marker pen. UV marking fades, especially when exposed to sunlight, so you will need to redo it from time to time. Marker pens are sold at stationers and DIY stores.

**Microdots** This type of property marking consists of pinhead sized microdots, each of which carries the same, unique code number – or a home postcode – and a central property registration telephone number for matching stolen goods with their owners. The system can be used to protect almost anything as the dots (which can be read under a microscope) are small and unobtrusive. Because the dots are hard to spot, a thief can never be certain that he has removed them all from a stolen item. This makes the system both an effective deterrent to theft, and a helpful tool for quickly identifying the rightful owners of stolen property.

Householders can obtain microdots through Neighbourhood Watch schemes and police Crime Prevention Panels. A kit contains approximately 1000 microdots and costs around £30.

---

### MARK AND MAKE AN INVENTORY

Decide what you value most and what might be attractive to thieves. Make a dated list of marked items as you mark them and take photographs at the same time. Whenever you buy new valuable items for the house mark these, too, and add them to your inventory.

# Bogus callers

Some thieves break in; others try to talk their way in and steal your property whilst you are distracted. These so-called bogus callers often claim to be on official business.

Typically, a bogus caller will claim to be acting for a gas, water, electricity or phone company, or the local council. Sometimes they pose as workmen carrying out emergency repairs. Another ruse is to say that their car has broken down and they need to phone someone for help. What they all have in common is that they are convincing and very persuasive.

## Distraction burglary

A burglary by a caller who gets into your home is known as a distraction burglary. There are around 12,000 such burglaries in the UK every year. The victims are often the elderly. You can avoid being a victim by taking certain precautions.

**Someone at the door** If the doorbell rings or there's a knock at your door, look out of your window to see who's there. If you don't recognise the caller, talk to them through the open window instead of going to the door. Or look through the spy hole viewer fitted in your front door. If you don't have a viewer, get one fitted; wide-angle viewers are available to help those with poorer eyesight.

**Put the door chain or door bar on** Before opening the door fully, use a door chain and talk to the caller through the gap.

### LOCK, STOP, CHAIN, CHECK

To try and help older people combat the problem of bogus callers, the government launched a campaign known as 'Lock, Stop, Chain, Check'. Local councils, social services and Age Concern centres all have information they can give older people; they will also help with door viewers, chains and mirrors. For the most vulnerable, they may be able to supply a personal attack alarm linked to a control centre.

Ask anyone who claims to be on official business to pass you their ID card. If you cannot read the card without your glasses on, close the door and go and get them. A genuine caller won't think that this is rude. If you still aren't sure, ask the caller to write and make an appointment, so you can arrange for someone to be with you when they come back.

**Set up a password** Most utility companies operate a password identification system. Phone your supplier if you would like to set up a password for confirming that meter readers are genuine.

**Stand your ground** Don't trust a caller who tries to distract you or get you to come outside – he or she may have a partner hiding ready to nip inside while your back is turned.

**Close doors behind you** If you come in from outdoors when someone knocks at your front door, take the time to lock the back door or shut the kitchen window before answering, in case the caller has an accomplice waiting to break in at the back of the house.

**Call the police** If you are at all worried by a caller, always phone the police.

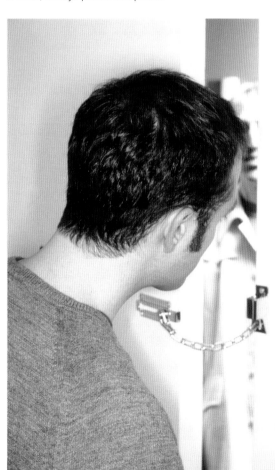

# Garages, sheds and outbuildings

Never store valuable items – such as a lawnmower or bicycles – inside an old wooden shed that may be easy for a thief to force open. Even garage doors may not be as strong as they look, so improve your security wherever you can.

An opportunist thief will not necessarily carry tools for breaking in, so will use anything he can spot lying around your property to force entry. After working outdoors, always put all your tools away and make sure that external buildings or storage caddies are securely locked. If you don't have secure storage outside keep tools indoors. Use specially designed ladder hooks to store ladders on an exterior wall, and secure them with a padlock and chain.

Make sure the bolts, locks and chains you use are strong enough for the job – some garden tools and furniture are highly prized to a thief. The best type of lock is a closed shackle, as it isn't possible to get a crowbar through the shackle to break it.

## Shed security

For sheds or garages with exterior door hinges, replace existing screws with security screws. These are designed so that they cannot be unscrewed once they have been screwed in. If your garage has double wooden doors, consider fitting a mortise lock with a rim latch. Fit a high-security padlock and secure the hasp with nuts and

bolts passing through the door and frame. Choose a hasp where the screw fixings are not accessible when it is locked (bottom) so that a thief cannot simply remove the entire lock to gain entry.

If you own any valuable garden tools or equipment, you can fit additional anchoring points (below) inside the shed or garage. These allow you to lock items using chains through eyebolts in the walls or floor.

Fix the anchor point in place using tamper-proof screws so that it cannot easily be removed, taking the tool you are trying to secure with it. Anchor points can also be concreted into a garage floor when the screed is laid or by digging out and replacing an area of concrete to make them even more secure.

Replace glass in shed windows with hard-to-break polycarbonate sheet, and fit window locks to any opening windows. Alternatively, an even more secure option is to simply screw windows shut from inside.

You can also buy security devices, such as a passive infra-red detector to detect motion and body heat, or a door contact system. Both of these will set off a siren if an intruder enters an outbuilding.

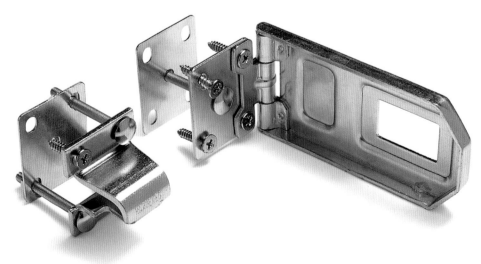

# Garage security

It is quite easy to break in through an inadequately secured up-and-over style garage door. An effective way to improve security is to fit a padlock with a hasp and staple on the inside. Another good system is the 'garage defender' lock. This type of lock acts like a foot pushed against the bottom of the door, preventing the up-and-over door's tilt action and making unauthorised access almost impossible.

A heavy-duty metal arm locks into a base plate that is bolted into the concrete outside the garage door.

If you are going on holiday, you can temporarily burglar-proof an up-and-over door on an integral garage by fixing a G-cramp onto each track immediately behind the door wheels. It will then be impossible to open the door from outside, even if the lock is successfully forced.

If you are more likely to enter your garage from inside your home, rather than from outside, you could fix bolts to the runners of an up-and-over garage door that can be locked from the inside.

## Connecting doors

If you have an integral garage, then it's vital that the door from the garage through into your house is secure (see pages 82–91). It should be as hard to breach as your main front door. A connecting door between the garage and the house is a secluded point of entry, popular with burglars – if they can break into your garage they will have time and privacy to spend forcing the internal connecting door.

---

## TOP TEN TIPS FOR OUTBUILDING SECURITY

Follow this advice to reduce the chance of having your garden tools and furniture stolen, and also to lower the chances of having your home broken into through your garden. Most burglaries happen via the back or side of the house, so these are precautions worth taking.

**1 Fit decent locks** Fittings should be bolted through the door and reinforced at the back with a steel plate. Any hasp should have concealed screws. Choose padlocks made of hardened steel no less than 60mm wide.

**2 Use an alarm** It's easy to fit battery operated alarms to the doors of any outbuildings.

**3 Fix it** Is there a cracked window in the shed or garage? Don't put it off: replace it, or make a strong temporary repair using plywood or polycarbonate sheet – not cardboard and duct tape – as soon as you notice it.

**4 Lock the windows** Fit window locks to any opening windows in garages and sheds; consider fitting grilles or heavy wire mesh.

**5 Keep it in view** A shed camouflaged by plants affords a great hiding place for a thief. Cut back dense foliage that might provide cover for an intruder.

**6 Secure tools and ladders** Don't make life easy for a thief by storing your tools outside. You can even secure tools and ladders together inside the shed or garage so that a burglar cannot use them without making a lot of noise trying to separate them.

**7 Put things away** Don't be tempted to leave tools and equipment out – even if you are just popping inside for a cup of tea part-way through a job. It takes seconds to steal something.

**8 Watch out** Ask neighbours to keep an eye on your house, garden and outbuildings and offer to do the same for them in return.

**9 Get insured** Upgrade your household contents insurance policy to include the shed, the garage and the equipment stored within them.

**10 Make a list** Keep a list of what you keep in the garage or shed, and mark your property (see page 108).

# Bicycle security

Bicycle theft is widespread, but you can reduce the risk of losing your bike by having it clearly marked as your property and by always using a good quality, heavy-duty bike lock.

Never leave your bicycle unlocked in a public place, even for a minute. At night, the best option is to store your cycle inside your home or garage: in fact your insurance company may only cover your bike if it's stored indoors overnight. Many offices offer secure indoor parking for cycling commuters, as do multi-storey car parks and this is probably safer than on-street parking.

If you don't have any choice, then try and find a proper cycle parking stand with rails that are securely bolted to the ground (below). The next best thing is 'street furniture' such as a lamppost or railings. Beware, though – some posts can simply be lifted out of the ground, while the cycle itself could be lifted off a parking meter or short signpost. Don't leave your bike on any railings where a sign prohibits bike parking, or it may be removed or double locked and you will have to pay to get it back.

Don't hide your bicycle out of view hoping that a bicycle thief will not notice it. It is far safer to lock it somewhere clearly visible to passers-by.

To help to recover your bicycle if it does get stolen, it is a good idea to take a photograph of your bike and make a note of its make, colour, serial number, frame number, model number and any other significant details. You will usually find the frame number underneath the bottom bracket, where the pedals are attached, or on the rear fork, where the back wheel slots in. Even better, register your bike with the Police Bike Register (see opposite).

## Choosing a bicycle lock

Lock strength varies, and you generally get what you pay for. While any lock can be broken, simply having a lock will deter the opportunistic thief. Even better, use a combination of two locks: one to secure easily removable wheels to the frame and the other to lock the frame to the railings or bicycle stand

**D-lock/U-lock** A rigid steel lock in a D or U shape. These look strong, but their strength can vary: the more you pay, the more secure the lock will be. D-locks are best

used along with another form of lock, such as a cable. Some come with attachments to fit them to the bike frame when they are not in use.

personal number combination that is not easy to guess.

**Chains and padlocks** Although they can be cumbersome and heavy to cart around, good quality chain and padlocks are the strongest option.

**Cable locks** Cables are flexible so can be used in situations where a D-lock might not fit. Cheap versions are easy to cut through, but they are a useful addition to a D-lock. Combination locks avoid the need for carrying a key, but remember to set a

**Click locks** Fixed to the bike near the seat post, they lock the rear wheel to the frame. Use only in combination with a lock that can fix your bike to an immovable object.

## LOG YOUR BICYCLE ONTO THE BIKE REGISTER

In the clampdown against bike theft, the police now support an online bike registration scheme at www.bikeregister.com. It costs £5.95 to register, then your bicycle's details are entered onto a police database – similar to the DVLA's log of car registrations and numbers – making it easy for police to identify and return stolen bikes. At the same time, you can also purchase a kit for visibly marking your bike or an electronic datatag to fit inside the frame for even greater security. A recent mass-marking campaign in London reduced bike theft by 75 per cent.

### Marking your bike

The bike register police-approved marking kit marks your frame with a telephone number and a unique code that identifies your bike's details on the database. Applying the kit yourself is an easy four-step process (below) that instantly makes your bike much less attractive to a thief.

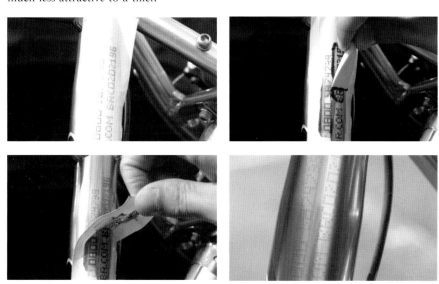

# Car crime

Car crime makes up nearly 20 per cent of all recorded crimes in England and Wales. Whether it is your car that is stolen or damaged, or contents taken from inside, it is distressing and inconvenient. Follow this advice to try to avoid becoming a car crime victim.

Every year, hundreds of thousands of cars are stolen and often never recovered. Often, a car that is recovered is badly damaged and has had the hi-fi, hands-free phone set, satellite navigation system and other equipment stolen. That is why you should regard the security features of your car as highly as any other feature.

Stolen cars will normally have their identity changed to make them easier to sell on. But you can help the police to identify the car as yours if you uniquely and invisibly mark it.

## Ultra-violet marking

Use an ultra-violet pen, which can be bought from any stationer's, to mark various parts of your car with the car's registration number. Think of places where you could mark your car that no thief would suspect. These might include the parts of the doors that are hidden when the door is closed, wheels, the back of the stereo and other equipment, such as DVD player head-units or multi-CD disc changers mounted in the boot, engine parts, the dashboard or any of the interior fittings.

## Glass etching

New cars are often etched with a unique security number. If yours isn't, then consider this option. A car thief will not want the

trouble and expense of replacing all the glass in your car, so get every window, mirror and the headlamps etched.

## Get an alarm fitted

Alarms can deter thieves not only from stealing your car, but also from taking things from it. Many modern cars are fitted with an alarm and immobiliser as standard equipment, but if yours is not, you can buy and fit a range of after-market options. At the very least, using a steering-wheel lock or a lock that prevents the gear stick and handbrake from being operated will act as a deterrent to opportunistic thieves.

You can find our more information about alarms, immobilisers and other security devices by phoning the Vehicle Security National Helpline on 0870 5502006 or the Sold Secure Helpline on 01327 264687.

## Additional security

Expensive alloy wheels are easy for a thief to sell on, but even standard wheels are easy pickings if they are not secure. Use locking wheel nuts – you only need one special nut on each wheel – which can only be removed with a special socket (below).

If your spare wheel is stored in a cradle beneath the car, find a way to lock this in place: these wheels are easy to remove in

---

### TAKE CARE OF YOUR KEYS

Don't leave your car keys on show in your house, so that a burglar getting into your home cannot easily take your car, too. Never leave them on a hall table that can be reached by feeding a cane through the letterbox (see page 77)

seconds and often a team of thieves will work their way up an entire street in one night stripping the spare wheels from every car they can.

Make sure that your fuel tank has a locking cap if the flap that hides it can be opened without the car key. This will prevent thieves from siphoning out your fuel – another common petty crime. And when you park, tuck in your wing mirrors and put the aerial down if you can to discourage vandalism.

## Used car checks

It is your responsibility to make sure a vehicle you wish to buy hasn't been stolen. Check that the name on the V5 registration document matches the name of the seller and match up the vehicle number and chassis number stated on the car itself. You can find out more in the free leaflets, *The Car-Buyer's Guide* and *Steer Clear of Car Crime*, available from a DVLA local office, your local Police Crime Prevention Officer or by visiting www.direct.gov.uk

## Car cloning

If you start being issued with demands to pay parking fines or notices about unpaid congestion charges, which you know nothing about, the chances are someone else is using your registration mark and has 'cloned' your car.

Cloning means replicating the identity of a similar, but not stolen, car on the road. The thief finds a vehicle (yours) that matches the make, model and colour of a car they have stolen, and then copies the identity of your legal vehicle by fitting the stolen car with a number plate with your registration on it. Since you need to provide identification and documents to support that you are the car's owner to buy new registration plates, car cloners often steal the plates from your 'donor' vehicle.

If your number plates are stolen or you think your car has been cloned, contact the police, who will issue you with a crime number. Return any demands for fines that do not relate to you, quoting this number.

You should also write to the Driver and Vehicle Licensing Agency (DVLA), alerting them to the theft of your plates. They will put your correspondence on the vehicle's record for future reference and may issue you with a new registration mark if your car has been cloned.

## THEFT FROM CARS

It may not be your car that tempts a thief, but what you have left inside.

• Think about where you park your car. Look for well-maintained, well-lit car parks.
• Always lock all doors, close windows and the sun-roof when you leave the car. Items are often stolen from unlocked cars.
• Do not leave bags, jackets or anything else on view. If you need to leave anything of value in your car then stow it out of sight, although thieves in car parks often watch out for drivers moving bags into the boot.
• Remove the stereo if you can. Remove portable SatNav devices, including the support cradle and suction pad, which can alert thieves that the device itself may be in the glove box.
• Don't leave documents in the car. Vehicle registration documents and driving licences are valuable to a thief.

# Motorbikes

A staggering 34,000 motorcycles and scooters are stolen in the UK every year. By and large, motorbikes are taken by professionals, who simply break them down for spares, while scooters tend to be taken by joyriders and opportunist thieves.

80 per cent of the stolen motorbikes are taken from the owner's home; half the owners did not lock their bikes when they left them. If you have security devices, always use them. A disc lock (below) is a heavy-duty steel lock, which fits through your brake disc and prevents the wheel from turning.

Alternatively, a heavy-duty chain and padlock can be used to lock your bike to a lamppost, the frame provided in a motorcycle parking bay or any other convenient immovable object.

If you find locking the bike with a special lock inconvenient or time consuming, then fit an alarm or immobiliser. Even with a lock this is an effective additional safety device. Many insurance companies will offer a reduction in your premium if a recommended alarm and immobiliser system is fitted.

### Electronic tagging for motorbikes

An additional deterrent to a would-be thief and an aid to recovering your bike if it is stolen is to fit an electronic datatag. Three microchips are fitted to the bike – one in the fuel tank and one on each wheel – and you are provided with an etching solution and stencils to etch a unique identifying number to the glass of the mirrors and to the panels on the bike Your bike's details are then logged with the datatag company so that it can be identified even if the number plates are changed.

## Safe parking

If you can, always park your motorbike in a locked garage or behind solid, locked gates off the road overnight. If you have to park the bike outside then use a sturdy cover that covers the whole thing; a thief stealing to order tends to go for something he can identify quickly. Park somewhere visible and in good light and if you are in a public place, choose designated bike-parking bays over a secluded spot. Never leave your keys with the bike, even for a moment.

# Caravans and boats

Caravans and boats on trailers are often left parked in one place for weeks or months at a time, giving a thief plenty of time and opportunity to plan to steal them.

If you can, store caravans and trailers out of sight in a back garden. If you have side or rear access to your garden it is possible to remove fence panels for access when leaving or coming home. Alternatively, use solid gates that are securely locked, preferably from the inside, to make it difficult for theives to gain access. There are several devices you can use to keep caravans and trailers secure.

Take a note of the 17-digit VIN (vehicle identification number), which should be stamped onto a caravan chassis, and keep it somewhere safe. This will help to identify your caravan if it is stolen and subsequently recovered. Electronic tagging devices similar to those used for motorbikes (see opposite) will also act as a deterrent to thieves and improve the chances of recovering a stolen vehicle.

**Hitch locks** prevent caravans from being quickly coupled up and towed away. Some come with built-in tamper alarms.

**Anchor points** can be concreted into the ground on your driveway. Secure your caravan or trailer to the anchor point with a thick chain and quality padlock.

**Caravan alarms** will alert you if the caravan is being moved and can frighten off a thief.

**Wheel clamps** (above) are simple to use and can be fitted in seconds. They deter the opportunist thief as they take time to remove.

## BOAT SECURITY

Take boat security seriously. Thieves are attracted to all kinds of things on boats, from outboard motors and life rafts to expensive fishing gear. Radios, tools and personal items can all be taken – as can the boat itself. Follow these guidelines and avoid being an easy target.

**Keep your boat locked** when no one is on board, even for a short time.

**Use strong locks** on all hatches and entry points.

**Review security regularly** Fit an alarm and display a sticker to say that one is fitted.

**Lock valuables away** Make sure your cockpit lockers can be properly locked and think about having a strongbox down below. Don't leave anything valuable on display.

**Tidy up** Don't leave anything loose in the cockpit or on deck.

**Take care of your keys** Don't leave your key in the ignition – always take it with you. And don't keep your boat keys on the same key ring as your engine keys.

# Security for an empty house

Unoccupied properties are an easy target for burglars. Minimise your risk of break-ins when you go away by making your home look lived in.

If you live in a detached house in a rural area backing onto farmland, you are at greater risk of burglary than if you live in a fourth floor flat in a modern, well-maintained block. In either case, though, your best allies in the fight against crime are other people.

Tell a member of your family, local friend or trusted neighbour that you plan to go on holiday. Give them details of when you are leaving and when you expect to be home. Ask them to carry out routine tasks, such as popping in every day and keeping the front garden looking neat, tidy and cared for. Get them to close curtains and blinds at night and open them in the morning. These activities will make it appear that the house is being used.

One tried and trusted way to check for occupancy is to look through a letterbox: a build-up of post lying on the doormat is a sure sign that no-one's home. Ask your friend to pick up the post every day and put it out of sight. Alternatively, sign up for

the Royal Mail's 'Keepsafe' service, which will keep your mail for up to two months while you are away.

An empty driveway can also be a giveaway that the homeowners are away. Ask a neighbour to leave a car parked in your drive or let them know that visitors to their house are free to use it for a while.

## Before you go away

There is no more obvious clue to an empty house than a build-up of milk and newspapers on the doorstep. Cancel all deliveries for the period you are away and ask a neighbour to push free newspapers right through the door and to pick them up with the post inside every day or so.

A house that is dark right round the clock is an obvious target. Fit time switches to operate lights, radios, televisions or other appliances for an hour or two at an appropriate time of day to make it look and sound as though there is someone home. Don't close your curtains – closed curtains in daytime are a good indicator that the house is empty.

Cut the lawn before you go so that it does not look neglected while you are away and trim back any plants that burglars could hide behind as they try to gain entry to your house.

Before you leave, move flat computer monitors, plasma TVs, laptop computers, iPod docking stations and other valuable, portable equipment to positions where they cannot easily be seen from a window.

Remember to give an emergency contact telephone number to the people looking after your home, and offer to return the favour whenever they go away.

Avoid talking about holiday plans in public places – you never know who's listening – and never write your home address on luggage labels while travelling. These can be read by anyone passing or standing behind you in a check-in queue and passed on to an accomplice who will then know that your house is going to be empty.

## Holidays at Christmas

One in four homes are left empty for at least one night between Christmas and New Year. Brand new goods bought as presents are irresistible to thieves, so this time of year presents rich pickings. One study found that British homes are 13 per cent more likely to be burgled during December than during any other month. You can minimise the risk of break-in by keeping unopened presents out of view and by putting new electronic goods away in a cupboard when you leave the house. If you are buying high-value gifts for members of the family, remember to add them to your insurance policy list if appropriate as soon as you buy them.

## House sitting services

If you are going away for any longer than a few days, you might want to consider paying someone to live in your house. Many home and contents insurance policies become null and void if your home is empty for 30 consecutive days and if you have pets, a live-in sitter can look after them, helping to offset kennelling costs.

The house sitter will also be on hand to organise repairs in the event of an emergency during your absence.

### YOUR HOLIDAY CHECKLIST

Use the following list as a basis for your own customised version of arrangements to make and things to check each time you go away.

- ✓ Newspapers cancelled
- ✓ Milk cancelled
- ✓ Neighbourhood Watch coordinator informed
- ✓ No one-off, mail-order deliveries expected
- ✓ Royal Mail 'Keepsafe' service activated to suspend post delivery if going away for several weeks.
- ✓ Travel plans left with friend or relative
- ✓ List made of all traveller's cheque numbers, and stored separately from cheques themselves
- ✓ List made of all credit card numbers, and stored separately
- ✓ Mobile phone number given to anyone who may need it
- ✓ Set of house keys left with friend or relative
- ✓ Heating turned down or off according to season
- ✓ Automatic light timer set; radio timer set to play on a mainly 'talk' station
- ✓ Appliances turned off (don't forget water-softener and immersion heater)
- ✓ Computers, TVs, microwave unplugged
- ✓ Modem line from computer unplugged
- ✓ Houseplants watered
- ✓ Perishable food items frozen or thrown away and food supplies in stock for when you get back
- ✓ Bins emptied
- ✓ Answering machine on
- ✓ Security lights set
- ✓ All windows locked
- ✓ All doors, including garage doors, side gates and sheds, locked
- ✓ Burglar alarm set

# Neighbourhood watch

Getting together with your neighbours to take action can have a dramatic effect on cutting local crime. Neighbourhood Watch schemes (or Home Watch as it is known in some areas) are not about taking policing into your own hands, but forming an active partnership with the local police force.

A Neighbourhood Watch scheme can be large – covering most of the households on an estate – or small, involving just a handful of properties in a country hamlet. Whatever its size, it gives people the reassurance that their neighbours are keeping an eye on each other's property as part of the strategy to reduce local crime rates – but that is not all. The scheme also brings together local people to create a sense of community and can be a powerful tool in tackling local problems with antisocial behaviour.

Members of a local scheme may decide to target local problems such as vandalism or graffiti. Perhaps a group will take positive action against burglary, such as helping one another to upgrade locks in vulnerable homes or for elderly residents who cannot do it themselves, or by lobbying the local authority to improve street lighting or prune overgrown bushes where car thieves or muggers can hide.

Dog fouling, fly tipping and abandoned vehicles can all become problems in an area, particularly if they are not tackled promptly. Research shows that areas that appear run-down and neglected are more likely to attract further problems than clean, well-kept streets. Neighbourhood Watch schemes can advise members on the legislation relating to dog fouling, fly tipping and abandoned vehicles, tell them how best to report the problem to the relevant agencies and suggest ways to prevent it. It is never a good idea to tackle someone directly if you see them dumping rubbish on the roadside, nor to attempt to

clear the rubbish yourself, but the main Neighbourhood Watch website has clear guidelines on what you can do.

### Building a community
An active Neighbourhood Watch scheme can be empowering, helping a community to believe that it can make a difference and tackle at least some of its problems. It helps people to feel less alone and afraid. Many schemes work in partnership with other agencies such as Help the Aged or Victim Support to provide additional help and advice, and counselling for victims of crime if they want it.

Neighbourhood Watch schemes play an important educational role, informing members about the latest crime prevention ideas to help them to keep their homes and possessions safe. Sometimes, membership of a scheme can even lead to reduced household contents insurance premiums.

## Setting up a scheme

A Neighbourhood Watch scheme is usually run by a volunteer co-ordinator; a larger scheme will probably have a committee as well. The committee meets regularly to discuss the problems that need tackling, and keeps in close touch with the local police to share information and advice. They will be able to alert scheme members if there is a spate of burglaries or car crimes in their area, or if bogus callers (see page 109) are working in nearby streets operating a scam.

If you are interested in setting up a scheme in your area, visit the website www.neighbourhoodwatch.uk.com where you will find everything you need to get started. Participating homes will be given stickers to put up in windows to alert potential burglars that houses in the local area are part of a Neighbourhood Watch scheme, and your local council may also erect signs on lampposts (above right).

Security marking kits (see page 108), burglar alarms and other security devices are also available through the scheme and local police Crime Prevention Officers will visit houses to advise on weak points in their security. 60 per cent of burglaries involve access at the side or rear of the house, so making your garden secure is also important and the Crime Prevention Officer will be able to advise you.

---

## COCOONING A HOME THAT HAS BEEN BURGLED

Statistics show that once a home has been burgled, it is more likely to be burgled again than a home that hasn't previously been targetted. This tends to happen within a few weeks of the original crime – just as the insurance company has begun to replace your missing valuables.

Assuming the burglar hasn't been caught, whoever committed the original robbery knows the weak points in your home's security. So if you are burgled, the first thing to do is upgrade the security.

Meanwhile, during the high-risk period immediately after a break-in, your Neighbourhood Watch scheme can form a protective cocoon around your home – a simple strategy that has been shown to lessen significantly the likelihood of a second attempt on the property. This involves immediate neighbours being especially watchful of your home for a few weeks, and reporting anything suspicious to the police.

# Student safety

Did you know that, statistically, students are one of the most likely groups to fall victim to crime? This is partly because they own more expensive consumer goods per head than the rest of the population.

A staggering one-in-three students becomes the victim of a crime each year. Students these days have computers, laptops, mobile phones, iPods and all sorts of other gadgetry that is easy to steal and, equally, easy to sell.

The crimes mostly likely to affect students are mugging, vehicle-related theft and burglary. Don't let your student son or daughter become another statistic. Make sure they are aware of their vulnerability, and before they go to college, give them this list of tips to help them to stay safe.

## Top safety tips

• In a hall of residence, be careful who you let in or who follows you into the building. Lock your bedroom door even if you are only going down the corridor.
• In a private rented home or flat, lock up windows and doors whenever you go out. If there is a lock on your bedroom door, make sure you use it.
• If possible, only use cash machines during daylight. Put your card and cash away promptly and never write down your PIN. Don't have the same PIN for all your cards, if you have more than one, and avoid choosing a number that is easy to guess, such as your year of birth or a consecutive sequence, such as 1234.
• Keep a note of your card details so you can cancel them quickly if they do get stolen.
• Always lock your car and put valuables out of sight; never leave the keys in the ignition, even if you're only paying for petrol.
• Don't leave your drink on a table or on the bar where it could be spiked or otherwise tampered with: hold on to it.
• Don't make yourself an easy target. At night, walk in groups, and after a night out travel home by taxi or stay with friends.
• Take care when using your mobile and try to avoid walking as you talk, as you will be distracted and less likely to notice someone approaching from behind to grab your phone. If your phone is stolen, call the

network straight away to immobilise it.
• Get insurance; note down the make, model and serial numbers of any electronic goods you have in case they are stolen.
• If you buy a new gadget or piece of expensive electronic equipmment – a flat screen for your computer or a new iPod, say – then don't leave its empty box outside your flat for burglars to see.
• Mark your property with your student ID number and the initials of your university (such as NU if you're at Newcastle). This makes your stolen goods harder to sell and makes it more likely that they will be returned to you if they are found.
• In the holidays take valuable items home, or ask your university if they have any secure storage facilities.
• If you have to leave valuables behind, make sure they cannot be seen through any windows.
• When you and your housemates go home for holidays, set timer switches (they cost as little as £2 each) to turn on lamps and radios, so that the house still looks occupied.

# Protect yourself from identity theft

Identity theft is a growing problem. Criminals who obtain other people's personal information can use even the most mundane of personal details to help them to 'verify' that they are someone they are not.

One of the most common ways of obtaining personal details is 'bin-raiding'. 75 per cent of local authorities admit that this happens regularly in their area. Certain simple precautions can reduce your risk. For example, before you throw away anything containing personal information – utilities bills, credit card receipts, special offers from loan agencies – make sure that you rip them up, or better still, shred them, so that prying eyes cannot read them or decipher any of the information they contain.

Another popular trick is to dupe you into giving personal information either in person, over the phone or via official looking e-mails.

## Protect your PC

Personal computers can hold plenty of information that is useful to fraudsters. The widespread use of wireless home networks connected to always-open broadband services make hacking into personal computers a simple task if you are not adequately protected. Install personal firewall software on your PC so that you can keep control of exactly who has access to your system and be diligent about keeping your software up-to-date, so that it does not become vulnerable to new hacking techniques and viruses that can infiltrate your data.

## Be careful who you talk to

Always be suspicious of anyone asking for what you think is too much personal information. Don't be afraid to challenge someone by asking why they need certain details. If they are a genuine caller they will be happy to explain, but if you are still not satisfied, call them back through the main customer service number of the company they claim to represent. Remember that a bank will never ask for your PIN, a whole security number or for your whole password.

Be suspicious if someone rings you – particularly on your mobile telephone – and then asks you to key in your number as confirmation. If they have called you legitimately then they already know your number; otherwise it may be a scam to use your phone's connection to make calls that will be charged to your bill.

Keep vital documents, such as your birth certificate, National Insurance number, receipts and bank statements, in a safe place. And if you think you have become the victim of identity thief, report it to the police immediately.

## Top tips to avoid becoming a victim

### Personal information

The Home Office advises that you regularly obtain a copy of your personal credit file to see which financial organisations have accessed your details. This is especially important in the first couple of months after moving house. Visit the websites of Experian, Call Credit or Equifax for more information.

If you live in a flat where other people might have access to your mail, consider asking your bank or credit card company to arrange for you to collect new cards or cheque books from a local branch.

If you move house, tell your bank, card issuer and all other organisations that you deal with immediately. For a small fee, the Post Office will redirect any mail to your new address for a specific period.

Keep all personal documents, such as your passport, driving licence and birth certificate, in a safe place, preferably in a lockable drawer or cabinet.

### Bank accounts and credit cards

If your cards are lost or stolen, cancel them immediately. Keep a note of the emergency numbers you should call and see the Card Watch website for more information.

When giving card details or personal information over the phone, internet or in a shop, make sure that others cannot see or hear your personal information. Shield the keypad when punching in your PIN at a cash point or till and beware of 'shoulder surfers' who may be watching from behind you. Choose a PIN that is not easy to guess and never use the same number for all your different cards. Likewise, use different passwords for different accounts.

Check card statements as soon as they arrive. If you spot anything you don't recognise, contact the card company immediately.

# Keep children safe online

It is important not to frighten children, but they need to know that – while the internet is full of new and interesting people to chat to – not everything you read is true, and not everyone you meet is who they say they are.

You may not be very confident about using computers and your children or grandchildren might be far more expert than you when it comes to navigating the net. That doesn't mean that you cannot give them good advice. Ask your children to show you some of their favourite sites, so you know what they are visiting.

### Stranger danger
Whatever you might have read or heard about stranger danger online, you don't need to ban your kids from using internet chat rooms to keep them safe. Children of all ages enjoy chat rooms, so before you ban them, try using chat rooms yourself and see how much fun they can be.

### Filtering software
Agree which chat sites your children can use and bookmark them to make them easy to access. Make children feel confident enough to come to you for help if they see or read anything that worries or frightens them. If a child has a bad experience – such as someone sending him nasty e-mails – he needs to be able to tell you about it and to know it's not his fault. It is a good idea to install filtering software such as Cybersitter, Netnanny or Safesurf, which will block unsafe websites and chat rooms.

### Keep it public
Make sure that children restrict their use to public chat rooms and always keep information about themselves and their family a secret. If they do want to chat with someone special, or even meet them, then they must tell you about it first. Remember that – as always with children – issuing an outright ban is unlikely to be effective, particularly with teenagers. If you do this, a meeting might happen anyway, but in secret – which could prove very dangerous indeed.

---

## SAFE CHATTING: TEN TOP TIPS

Copy this list out, bright and bold, and pin it next to the computer. Talk through the points on the list regularly with your children.

**1** Enjoy chatting with your friends online, but be careful who you trust.

**2** Keep your address, telephone number, and personal information a secret – even if you trust the person you're chatting with.

**3** Treat your friends' and family's personal information with the same secrecy.

**4** Always use a nickname instead of your real name when chatting or instant messaging.

**5** Never use private one-to-one chat rooms; stick to the public ones.

**6** If you begin chatting to someone regularly, tell an adult friend or a parent what you are doing.

**7** Always tell an adult friend or parent if you receive a rude or nasty message on the internet – it's not your fault, so don't feel bad.

**8** Never meet with anyone you get to know online unless an adult friend or parent comes with you.

**9** Check with an adult or parent before you send a picture of yourself over the internet.

**10** Treat other people online the way you like to be treated; don't be nasty or rude.

# Acknowledgments

**All images in this book are copyright of the Reader's Digest Association Limited, with the exception of those in the following list.**

*The position of photographs and illustrations on each page is indicated by letters after the page number:*
T = Top; B = Bottom; L = Left; R = Right; C = Centre

The majority of images in this book are © Reader's Digest and were previously published in Reader's Digest *DIY Manual*, *1001 DIY Hints and Tips*, *How Everything in the Home Works* or *First Aid*

**2** iStockphoto.com/Anna Sirotina **10–11** iStockphoto.com/Winston Davidian **26 L** iStockphoto.com/Khanh Trang **42 TR** www.safelincs.co.uk (Freephone 0800 0776149) **BL** iStockphoto.com/Duncan Babbage **44 TR** iStockphoto.com/MorganLane **BL** iStockphoto.com/Sergey Kashkin **45 T** ASTA BEAB Certification Services Ltd www.astabeab.com **B** ASTA BEAB Certification Services Ltd www.astabeab.com **46 TR** Getty Images Ltd/David Seed Photography **BL** iStockphoto.com/Christoph Riddle **47 TR** www.safelincs.co.uk (Freephone 0800 0776149) **BL** Corbis/Pat Doyle **BR** www.safelincs.co.uk (Freephone 0800 0776149) **49 T** iStockphoto.com/René Mansi **B** iStockphoto.com/Olivier Blondeau **53 T** iStock photo.com/Steffen Siegrist **C** iStockphoto.com/Matej Michelizza **B** Jupiter Images **56** Alamy Images/MasPix-Backgrounds **59 BR** Science Photo Library/Chris Priest **62 R** www.grassnake.co.uk **63** Alamy

Images/Chuck Pefley **65 BR** www.trampledunder-foot.co.uk **70** Rex Features Ltd/Garo/Phanie Red Cover/© Keith Scott Morton **74** Alvey & Towers Picture Library iStockphoto.com/slobo mitic **77 TR** Punchstock/Stockbyte/George Doyle **78–79** iStockphoto.com/Joseph Jean Rolland Dube **100 C** Yale UK **103 R** Rex Features Ltd/Steve Meddle **108** 0 Rex Features Ltd/Shout **109** Corbis/Dennis Cooper/Zefa **110 T** www.torc-anchors.com **111** SAS Security Products Ltd **112 T** iStockphoto.com **B** Alamy Images/Steven May **113 TL, TR** Jupiter Images **CL, CR, BL, BR** www.bikeregister.com **114 T, B** Alvey & Towers Picture Library **115 T** © Photofusion/Bob Watkins **B** Alamy Images/Nick Lewis Photography **116 TL, BR** Alvey & Towers Picture Library **BL** Alamy Images/© Plainpicture GmbH & Co.KG **117 TR** Alvey & Towers Picture Library **BL** Alamy Images/© Paul Thompson Images **119** iStockphoto.com/Dave White **121 TR** © Photofusion/George Montgomery **B** www.neighbourhoodwatch.uk.com **122** Alamy Images/Peter Titmuss **124** iStockphoto.com/Lisa Eastman

Reader's Digest *Home Safety & Security DIY Manual* is based on material in Reader's Digest *DIY Manual*, published by The Reader's Digest Association Limited, London.

First Edition Copyright © 2007
The Reader's Digest Association Limited,
11 Westferry Circus, Canary Wharf,
London E14 4HE
www.readersdigest.co.uk

**Editor** Alison Candlin

**Art Editor** Kate Harris

**Assistant Editors** Helen Spence and Diane Cross

**Editorial Consultant** Mike Lawrence

**Proofreader** Rosemary Wighton

**Indexer** Marie Lorimer

### Reader's Digest General Books

**Editorial Director** Julian Browne

**Art Director** Anne-Marie Bulat

**Managing Editor** Alastair Holmes

**Head of Book Development** Sarah Bloxham

**Picture Resource Manager** Sarah Stewart-Richardson

**Pre-press Account Managers** Penny Grose and Sandra Fuller

**Senior Production Controller** Deborah Trott

**Product Production Manager** Claudette Bramble

**Origination** Colour Systems Limited, London

**Printed and bound** in China by CT Printing

The contents of this book are believed to be accurate at the time of printing. However the publisher accepts no responsibility or liability for any work carried out in the absence of professional advice.

We are committed to both the quality of our products and the service we provide to our customers. We value your comments, so please feel free to contact us on 08705 113366, or via our website at www.readersdigest.co.uk

If you have any comments about the content of our books, email us at gbeditorial@readersdigest.co.uk

Reader's Digest would like to thank Adelice Cross-Ashworth for permission to use the illustrations on page 49.

ISBN: 978 0 276 44203 2
BOOK CODE: 400-339 UP0000-1
ORACLE CODE: 250011348S.00.24